Under the General Editorship of

Jesse W. Markham, Princeton University

Houghton Mifflin Adviser in Economics

SOVIET
ECONOMIC
POWER

ROBERT W. CAMPBELL

wellington

INDIANA UNIVERSITY

Its Organization,

Growth, and Challenge

SECOND EDITION

HOUGHTON MIFFLIN COMPANY · BOSTON

New York · Atlanta · Geneva, Ill. · Dallas · Palo Alto

COPYRIGHT © 1966, 1960 by Robert W. Campbell.

PRINTED IN THE U.S.A.

Editor's Introduction

Editor's Introduction

Since the beginnings of civilized man crucial debate has been waged over the issue of which powers should reside in government and which should be retained by the individual members of society. Throughout the past two decades the United States and the Soviet Union have customarily been singled out as occupants of opposing poles in the broad spectrum of resolutions to this debate. In the United States great stress is laid on the ballot box and the free market mechanism; in the Soviet Union the emphasis is on political authority and central planning.

In such a world it is inevitable that other countries, especially the so-called "uncommitted" countries, meticulously compare the more visible performance indexes of the two social systems. In truth, this rivalry often resembles the athletic drama enacted in the representative college stadium throughout the United States during the football season. Sputnik I and the first moon shot brought cheers from the Soviet camp and extravagant claims for the superiority of socialistic science. And the equally impressive accomplishments of United States space men were met with applause from those nations who identify their interests with the free world.

While it is inevitable that the United States and the Soviet Union be compared by other nations, it is absolutely necessary, both for them and to the rest of the world, that each of these powerful nations devote careful and meticulous study to the other. United States-Soviet relationships hang not only on developments in each of the two countries, but also on how well developments in one are understood in the other.

Professor Campbell's *Soviet Economic Power* has been widely acclaimed since its publication in 1960 for the contribution it has made to understanding the Soviet economy. Since his original training in this field at the Russian Research Center of Harvard University, he has done research on many aspects of the Soviet economy. His enviable capacity for clear and incisive writing enabled him to communicate his knowledge of the subject to others. The result was a book read profitably by the professional economist, social scientists, and the intelligent citizen regardless of their professional or vocational classification.

Professor Campbell's first edition identified important changes which had occurred in the Soviet Union and concluded with a chapter on the Soviet economy's future prospects. Here and there he made highly illuminating comparisons between United States and Soviet economic indexes. In the intervening five years a fraction of the future in 1960 has entered the historical record; significant changes have occurred in both the Soviet Union and the United States; and the economic indexes of 1960 require updating. Meanwhile, at a global level, relationships between the Soviet Union and the United States, and between each of these and other nations, have undergone observable change. It can now be argued persuasively that Communist China may even have displaced the Soviet Union at the far authoritarian end of the spectrum. This development, along with others of equal moment, have given rise to considerable speculation that the United States and Soviet economies are gradually losing some of their harshest dissimilarities. Professor Campbell has captured all this in the revised edition of his *Soviet Economic Power*. Those familiar with the first edition will welcome the revised version with enthusiasm. Those who are not will find the revised version a clear and exciting introduction to the Soviet economy.

JESSE W. MARKHAM

PRINCETON UNIVERSITY

Preface

Any description of Soviet economic institutions is subject to rapid obsolescence. Also, since the history of the Soviet experiment in forced industrialization goes back for only a third of a century, the unfolding of another decade or even five years of experience can greatly alter our overall perspective on it. Since the appearance of the first edition of this book in 1960, the Russian leaders have several times reorganized the machinery by which their planned economy is administered, and have been groping toward a new and more rational understanding of the economic process and new notions about the goals their economy ought to serve. Behind these changes lies an urgent search for some way to counteract the marked deterioration in economic performance that the Soviet system has experienced since the late fifties. Outside the Soviet Union, much new research on the Soviet economy has been completed since the first edition, making possible a significant increase in our knowledge of the details and the explanation of Soviet growth performance in the past. In combination with the recent deceleration of growth, this fuller picture has produced some changes in our interpretation of the Soviet "growth machine," and in our evaluation of the future growth capabilities of the system. In addition to bringing the description of the Soviet economy up to date, the second edition differs from the first in seeing the economic rivalry of the Soviet Union in less starkly threatening terms.

In the few years since the first edition there have been great changes in the level of sophistication of Soviet economic thought. A revolution in economic theory, stemming mostly from the work of V. V. Novozhilov and L. V. Kantorovich, has overthrown most of the Marxian ideological roadblocks which once hampered the ability of Soviet planners and economists to understand economic issues and to think fruitfully about making the behavior of planners and production organizations more rational and efficient through economic reorganization. No less startling has been a change in the pronouncements of Soviet leaders about priorities. The old policy of giving precedence to the goals of planners over those of the population has been called into question. There is now much discussion about how properly to balance off the desires of consumers for more here and now against the use of resources to promote goals favored only by the leaders. Kosygin, for one, has stated unequivocally that the share of national income devoted to consumption ought to be increased. So far, however, these movements for change have not much altered the traditional features of the Soviet economy. The consumer seems more favored in speeches than in the figures of the new Five Year Plan, and the implications of the new economics for possible reorganization of the mechanisms by which producers are motivated and controlled are but poorly seen by the leaders or even by many economists. Despite incessant institutional tinkering, retreat from the distinguishing feature of the Soviet system, i.e., its high degree of centralization, or movement from the principle of administrative guidance to that of price guidance, has been imperceptible. Despite the present atmosphere of incipient change, the system changes very slowly, and my approach has been to concentrate on the system as it is today, to show the kinds of difficulties and problems it encounters, and to analyze the possible impact of proposed changes, rather than to predict the extent or speed of change.

This revision contains several changes in the organization of the material. I have tried to integrate the various elements of Soviet growth policy into something like a coherent strategy of growth, and to interpret the effectiveness of this strategy against the background of place and circumstance. This also makes it easier to consider the possible application of the Soviet approach to growth to other developing countries. Also I have tried to highlight and integrate more effectively the discussion of the central issue of how resources get allocated in the Soviet economy by focussing on the theme of economic decision making as it appears in various contexts. This approach also makes it possible to consider in a more fundamental and theoretical way the divergent approaches the Russians have employed in different parts of the system, and to think more clearly about the possible inroads that marketization might make on the system. Incidentally, this approach also provides a very helpful framework for discussing the fundamental issues of agricultural policy and of foreign trade, the latter a subject treated more explicitly in this edition than in the first.

The Suggestions for Further Reading at the end has been retained, but the large change in its contents is witness to the rapidity with which new developments and research have occurred in this field. The factual information and many of the ideas in this book are products of the efforts of many people, and I want to express my appreciation especially to the authors of the works cited in the list of Suggestions.

ROBERT W. CAMPBELL

INDIANA UNIVERSITY

Contents

Soviet Economic Power

1

Introduction

The contemporary world presents two radically different models for a modern, dynamic society. One, the Soviet-type society, is based on an economic system that is planned, highly centralized, authoritarian. The other, of which the United States is the familiar prototype, is based on an economic system that is market-coordinated, decentralized, consumer-directed. The differences between the two societies extend far beyond their economic organization, of course. Indeed, it is in the political and moral spheres that the contrast and conflict between them is the sharpest. The present book, however, is concerned primarily with their economic organization and behavior.

The relative power and influence of these two types of economy have changed dramatically in the past thirty-five years. In 1928, at the beginning of the Soviet drive for industrialization, the Soviet-type economy was confined to the Soviet Union and, in terms of absolute levels of output and the productivity of its resources, it represented a very backward economic system. It had a vast land area and natural resources and a population of some 150 million persons but these resources were poorly utilized and Great Britain, with a population one-fourth as large, had an industrial output about four times as great. This situation has changed sharply. As a result of three and a half decades of forced industrialization, the Soviet Union surpasses all the former industrial gi-

1

ants of Western Europe in terms of industrial output and now stands
second only to the United States. It produces more steel, more
electric power, more coal than any of the Western European
countries. Moreover, the territorial expanse in which this form of
economic organization operates has widened greatly. The Soviet
Union with the aid of military power has extended its own borders
and is now ringed by socialist regimes in six countries along its
European border. The magnitude of this expansion is indicated by
the population living in the new areas, i.e., more than 100 million
persons. Soviet-type societies have also come to power in China
and in several small Asian countries — encompassing perhaps
another 600–700 million persons. In Stalin's time, all these countries copied fairly closely the economic institutions of the Soviet
Union and adopted policies to achieve rapid growth rather similar
to those of the Soviet Union. There has now arisen considerable
diversity within this Soviet world in matters of economic organization and policy as well as in ideologies and political objectives.
Some of the East European countries have retreated in appreciable
degree from the extreme centralization of the Soviet model. China,
whose development effort had to contend with a more backward
economy and a less favorable resource position than had existed
in Russia, has introduced several innovations in the Soviet development strategy. These differences within the bloc are quite important (and of great interest) but since our goal in this book is to
explain Soviet economic organization and growth, we will have
little opportunity to consider them carefully.

Whether the coexistence of these two systems occurs in a peaceful setting or in one of conflict, there is inevitably a strong rivalry
between them. The Russians hold as an article of faith that their
economic system represents the wave of the future, that it is a
"progressive" economic system that will in time everywhere sup-
plant the outmoded, historically doomed capitalist system. This
faith implies a certain hostility toward us, as indicated in the famous boast by Khrushchev that he expected to bury the capitalist
system and that our grandchildren would live under Soviet socialism. This idea is grounded in an elaborate official orthodoxy and
is propagandized with evangelical zeal. It is not solely an official
view; it is probably held also by most Soviet citizens. Americans,
albeit with a less elaborate and less consciously formulated ideol-

ogy, believe that our type of economic system is the ultimate in efficiency, in satisfying the needs of the people, in stimulating technical progress, and in meting out economic justice. To the extent that there are imperfections in the American system, these can gradually be eliminated or remedied without modifying its essential nature. They see no reason why our type of economy cannot continue to function in the future as it has in the past.

These respective faiths are, of course, an essential requirement for the operation of the economic system in each country. They are part of what it takes to assure commitment and dedication on the part of the participants in the systems. But the target to which these ideologies are addressed is coming to be more and more the citizens of the underdeveloped and uncommitted countries of the world. Measured in terms of people, land area, economic potential, etc., much of the world is still outside either of the two types of economic system described. Economically, these underdeveloped areas remain in a pre-modern state — unproductive and poverty-ridden. Peoples in this situation have become aware of their status and, what is more important, want to change it. They are determined to shake off the stagnation of the past and to move onto the road of dynamic industrialism. They want the benefits of high consumption, urbanization, education, leisure, and better health which industrialization brings. Most of these countries are now in the process of making choices about how their economic life is to be reorganized, and one of the important areas of competition between the Soviet type and the free-enterprise type of economic system is in winning emulators among the underdeveloped countries.

The message which the United States has for them is that if they want enough to eat, hospitals, some relief from backbreaking toil, and ultimately refrigerators, shopping centers, and color television, they need only to reconstruct their societies along the lines of our model. If they adopt our institutions — private property, laissez-faire, political democracy, private investment — and adopt our values of ambition, the money calculus, belief in the dignity of work, commercial honesty, and others, they will find that the fruits we enjoy come in due time. The response to this message has not been overly enthusiastic. These ingredients of our system are too much the product of our special history, too elusive to be transplanted from outside into an alien environment. Furthermore, it sounds like too passive an approach to satisfy the impatience of peoples newly awakened to the possibilities that modern technology offers them.

The Russian line is a seductive one. The Russians suggest that the hope of abundance via the capitalist method is an illusion. Their argument might be paraphrased as follows:

What the capitalists of the advanced countries want is to keep your countries in a dependent position in order to exploit you. After all, the capitalist countries have been preaching their advice of emulation for a century or so, but what has happened? You are more impoverished than ever. If you want to develop, you need, rather, to follow the trail blazed by socialism in the Soviet Union. At the time of the .Revolution we too were a poor agrarian country, with low levels of consumption, exploited by foreign capitalists, with an uneducated population, backward by any index of social and economic development. But, guided by the teachings of the great leaders, Marx, Engels, Lenin, we found a way to break out of this economic stagnation. We overthrew the capitalists, nationalized all the means of production, set central planners in control of the entire economic life of the country. As a result of this radical transformation we have succeeded in industrializing at an unprecedented rate. Our success in raising output and creating modern industry put to shame the achievements of the bourgeoisie even in its heyday.

We have already overtaken those pioneers of the industrial revolution — England, France, Germany — and it is only a matter of time before we overtake the United States itself. Already in some fields we have demonstrated achievements far beyond anything the Americans have ever accomplished. Any backward country that wants to develop has only to copy our techniques of economic organization; our example shows the possibilities of the future for all who choose to follow it.

It matters little that this is a seriously distorted picture, that the sacrifices and failures of the Soviet system are never mentioned, that many dark corners of Soviet life have been omitted from this optimistic picture of the Soviet experience. The central theme, that the Soviet system has made it possible to achieve unprecedented rates of growth, is basically true and this is the telling point.

Moreover, the Soviet Union has now attained a level of economic power which enables it to press these appeals not only through the use of diplomacy, propaganda, and subversion but also through economic ties. The Russian leaders can use the instruments of economic aid, technical assistance, and trade to tighten the ties of underdeveloped countries with the Soviet economy. The importation of goods and technical assistance from the Soviet Union impresses on the citizens of those countries a picture of the Soviet Union as a world leader in matters of economics and technology and also serves as a means for developing more or less permanent economic dependency. To the extent that the growth of an underdeveloped country is based on grants or imports of Soviet machinery and Soviet technology, there will be a continuing relationship in the form of needs for replacement, spare parts, engineering advice, and markets for exports. Thus far the absolute amount of Soviet foreign assistance has been small compared with the resources which the United States government has given or lent abroad. Nevertheless, the Russian program of credit and technical assistance has only started — and it is growing rapidly. Moreover, it is concentrated in an area of the world where our efforts have been relatively slight. In twenty-eight underdeveloped countries — those to which the Soviet Union has extended aid — Soviet aid deliveries in the past few years have been about one-third as much as ours. In twelve of these countries, Soviet aid commitments exceed those of the United States, though much of this aid is still to be delivered.

In the background of such peaceful forms of competition there is an ever-present military rivalry. The Russians have managed to carry out a military program that gives them military strength approaching ours in many respects. Their ability to do this is based partly on the great increase in economic power brought by thirty-five years of industrialization. They have created a capability in matters of technology and a production base that makes possible the production in large volumes of the things needed in modern war. But Soviet ability to compete with us in military power is enhanced by the fact that their economic system makes it possible for them to divert to military purposes the amounts their leaders feel are required — without appealing to public support, as is necessary in our country. In comparison with ours, their ability to support a military program is much greater than would be indicated by the relative outputs of the two economies. With their steel, aluminum, electric power, and petroleum output much smaller than ours, they still find no difficulty in diverting to military uses amounts comparable to our own. Nevertheless, the most important danger which the existence of the Soviet Union poses for us is not its approach to us in military capabilities. Many would argue that in an age of nuclear weapons direct military aggression is not a feasible instrument of national policy and that the present situation will involve a long drawn-out military stalemate, with the conflict shifted to other grounds such as "guerrilla wars of liberation." The extension throughout the world of the Soviet economic system and the sort of society that goes with it would leave us stranded and isolated, an odd survival in the midst of a hostile, alien world. Massive military attack in such a situation would be superfluous.

This is an upsetting perspective but one that Americans will have to live with for a long time to come. Clearly it calls for more careful study and more complete understanding on our part of the Soviet economic system. From now on, we will be dealing constantly with problems arising from the operation of the Soviet economic system. The decisions we make for ourselves in education, foreign aid, military policy, and internal economic policy, to list only a few of the most critical areas, must be predicated on an intelligent understanding of what the Soviet economic system is like, how it works, and what it can do. And it is not just congressmen and administrators who must have this understanding — they will act only if supported, perhaps only if pushed, by informed public opinion.

The intent of this book is to provide a realistic picture of the Soviet economic system as a base for this understanding. Chapter 2 discusses the history of the Soviet economy in order to show the sort of considerations that lie at the foundations of their economic policy and to show the long-term commitment to economic growth which permeates their thinking. Chapters 3 through 5 explain how the Soviet economy operates. They describe the distinctive institutions and processes by which decisions are made about organizing production and allocating resources. Chapters 6 and 7 are devoted to a description of Soviet economic performance. They consider such questions as the rate of Soviet growth, the com-

parative sizes of United States and Soviet output, the allocation of
Soviet output among major uses, and how effectively the Soviet system utilizes the vast resources at its disposal. Chapter 8 contains
a summary interpretation of past Soviet performance in terms of the
main features of Soviet economic organization and a discussion of
the prospects for further growth and possible evolution of economic
organization and policy in the future.

2

Ideological and Historical Background

Basic to the investigation of any phenomenon is a framework of assumptions from which to work. To understand something like the Soviet economic system it is necessary to have some point of departure for studying it or even for thinking about it. We must inevitably have some preconception — perhaps only in the back of our minds — about the essential nature of the Soviet economic system. Since the assumptions or definitions from which we start will always confine our thinking, it is important to try to set up here at the beginning some sensible premise about "what kind of thing the Soviet economy is."

The Role of Marxism in Soviet Economics

If one asks a group of reasonably knowledgeable people for a characterization of the Soviet economy, many will answer to the effect that the Soviet economy is an attempt to apply the fallacious doctrines of Karl Marx to running an economy. This is not a very helpful point of departure. First of all, it does not carry one very far in interpreting Soviet life because few people have any notion of what the "fallacious doctrines" of Karl Marx are. How many have read and understood the three volumes of *Das Kapital?* The most serious deficiency of this interpretation, however, is that when people imprison themselves within it, they become preoccupied with connecting every act of the Soviet government with some Marxist idea. There is an urge to interpret everything as some logical result of the Marxist heritage or as a perfidious betrayal of Marx's real meaning. Such an exercise tends to be fruitless because the explicit theories and even the spirit of Marxist analysis are largely irrelevant to the conditions and problems of the Soviet situation. Marx's analysis was mainly concerned with the future development of nineteenth-century industrial capitalist countries — not with the task of propelling a peasant society into the twentieth century. Consequently there is no connection between much of what Soviet leaders think and do and the thought or writings of Karl Marx. It is true that the Soviet leaders take great pains to interpret and justify their acts by appeal to Marx, but as we hope to demonstrate further on, this is mostly in the nature of a rationalization after the fact. The vague Marxist goal of achieving communism is something they can make ritual obeisance to, but their motivations and preoccupations are connected with more immediate problems. Thus it is important at the very outset to reject consciously the formulation that the Soviet economy is applied Marxism and to formulate a new definition, a new point of departure. The one I would suggest is that *the Soviet economy is totalitarianism harnessed to the task of rapid industrialization and economic growth.* The purpose of the present chapter is to explain and document this conception of the nature of the Soviet economic system.

The Communist Party professes Marxism as its sacred official ideology. Great care is taken to preserve the sanctity of this ideology and to rationalize everything in terms of it or by appeal to it. But in a way this is all a monstrous pretense. It is probably fair to say that the triumph of a proletarian revolution in the Soviet Union was a great doctrinal mistake. Without trying to discuss the correctness of Marx's analysis of historical forces and his view of what causes historical change, we can certainly say that he was not even thinking about proletarian revolution for Russia. In his overall scheme of things the historical forces at work in Russia had not yet made it ready for socialism. The Bolsheviks did not win power in the Soviet Union because they followed the prescriptions of the science of Marxist socialism but because they ingeniously amended and modified his analysis. It was by introducing a strain of voluntarism into the Bolshevik version of Marxism that Lenin made the revolution a success. And he made it a success not because he acted on the basis of Marxist concepts and analysis but because he himself was a wonderfully creative political thinker and strategist. The Russian Communists were not brought to power because of the historically inevitable growth of working-class power which Marx supposed would accompany the maturation of capitalism but more or less completely in the absence of such development. They triumphed because of Lenin's ability to find a program that would keep the peasantry on his side, or at least neutral, and by his development of the Communist Party and of other organizational and institutional devices for manipulating and controlling political forces. Lenin and the Communist Party which he led were not made by the revolution — rather, they made the revolution.

When the Bolsheviks had achieved power they found themselves in an anomalous situation. By the lights of a good Marxist, they didn't really belong in power. The social basis for their power was absent; they had misinterpreted Marx and followed an adventurist policy. Nevertheless they held control of the country. Some of the Bolsheviks rationalized their situation by saying that the Russian Communists had perhaps prematurely moved out ahead on one front of the socialist struggle, but that the industralized countries would soon follow their lead. This would vindicate the Bolshevik revolution and remove the anomaly of their position. Others thought that they could not hope to preserve the full socialist revolution in Russia. They would make a heroic effort, point the way, then let their effort go down as a glorious, path-breaking example from which others might draw inspiration and guidance.

The events of the year or two after the revolution made it seem as if the socialist revolution in Russia could not endure. The hoped-for revolutions in the main capitalist countries did not materialize. The few socialist regimes that did come to power were soon overthrown and within the Soviet Union civil war and foreign intervention made the prospects for the survival of a socialist regime at home look somewhat doubtful. Even when the withdrawal of foreign troops and military victory in the civil war made the prospects look better, the Bolshevik regime came face to face with the opposition of the peasants, a problem which should not even exist for a true Marxist revolution. Presumably, in a country ripe for the socialist revolution, peasant agriculture would already have virtually disappeared. Actually, the peasants, no longer fearing the return of the previous landowning class, increased their resistance to the requisitions of agricultural produce which the Bolsheviks were demanding. When this happened, the Party faced the grim prospect of losing even the support of the small urban proletariat which it could no longer supply with food. When in 1921 the workers combined with the peasants in opposition to the Bolsheviks in the famous Kronstadt revolt, it was clear that the regime had lost the support of even its staunchest supporters. At this point it looked as though Russia was really not ripe for the triumph of a socialist revolution.

The New Economic Policy

But Lenin was more of a revolutionary than a doctrinaire Marxist logician and he was not prepared to sacrifice the revolution just because it looked as though the Marxist prerequisites for it were absent. Faced with the contretemps of the disaffection of the working class, in whose name he claimed to speak, he analyzed the situation carefully and then repudiated almost entirely the policies and approaches the regime had followed for three years. Beginning in March 1921, he introduced a series of decrees, described as the New Economic Policy (NEP), which restored a considerable measure of capitalism to the Soviet economy, particularly in agriculture and trade. His idea was that by this strategic retreat the party could keep control of the country but stimulate its recovery from the destruction and disorganization of the war years. Once the pressing problem of getting the economy functioning again was solved, the Party could then resume its advance toward socialism. And indeed it worked out as planned. The NEP was a success in terms of economic reconstruction and it gave party leaders a breathing spell in which to analyze their situation and canvass the possible routes along which they might proceed.

Consider the Party's position at this juncture. The Bolsheviks were supposedly a proletarian party whose power was based on the support of the industrial urban working class. But in fact the industrial working class scarcely existed in the Soviet Union at this point. Moreover, all their Marxist ideology had suggested that they would inherit an industrialized, highly productive country in which the workers were in the majority; a country in which the workers were accustomed to the discipline of an industrial society and had the skills of an industrial society; a country in which the people would be educated and urbanized. These were more or less esssential preconditions for ushering in the era of abundance that the socialist revolution was to bring. These conditions clearly did not exist in the Soviet Union. Consequently, the leaders were in a precarious position inside the country and in an even more precarious position in the world as a whole. The social class that was theoretically the basis of their political power scarcely existed and the level of economic development of their country made it very weak vis-à-vis the hostile capitalist powers. So if they decided to remain in power and preserve the socialist nature of their revolution, the logic of the situation clearly demanded that they create the prerequisites for their existence and survival. They had to effect a rapid industrialization, both in order to make their society one in which they would have political support and in order to become strong enough to defend themselves in the environment of a hostile and economically advanced capitalist world.

Obvious as this is from our point of view almost fifty years later, it was not completely understood at the time. For a while there was some argument about whether they should try to preserve socialism and it was some time before they completely convinced themselves that their survival depended on industrialization. Moreover, it was not completely clear to them that they would have to industrialize in a serious, large-scale way and that this task would pose almost insurmountable problems. Nevertheless, by the middle twenties there was agreement among the Bolshevik leaders on the possibility of remaining in power and on the need to industrialize.

The Great Industrialization Debate

Agreement on the need to embark on a program of industrialization and economic growth brought forward a whole series of other controversial issues. How were they to industrialize? How fast? Where would the resources come from? Around these questions there developed a serious debate.

These issues were central to many of the policy problems which the regime faced and constituted the principal substance of economic and political debate and maneuvering in the twenties.

The issues can probably be understood best if we pose them as a simple two-sided argument between rival factions in the Communist Party. To be sure, this is an oversimplified approach. Many of the protagonists were not consistent in their positions over time. They changed their arguments or changed the emphasis that they gave to different aspects of the arguments. Also there were more subtle differences not reflected in this simple dichotomy; there were other groupings of opinion besides the two main ones that we indicate here. Despite the disadvantages of posing the argument in this simple way, however, it is a good approach for understanding the essential problem.

The Rightist Position. One of the two main positions in this argument was that of the group identified as the moderates or Rightists who more or less controlled official government policy during the NEP. This group took the premises and rationale of the NEP as their point of departure. As we have already indicated, the NEP was a strategic retreat, an attempt to accommodate to the weakness of the Party vis-à-vis the peasants and also to a certain extent vis-à-vis the workers. During the period of War Communism that preceded the NEP the regime had gotten into an impasse in which it could retain the support of the workers and keep the urban economy going only by forcibly requisitioning grain from the peasants. But the regime was simply not powerful enough to pursue this policy indefinitely. The peasants had too many defenses. First of all, so many of the peasants were scattered over such a wide area that it was difficult to enforce demands for grain. Even if the Party mobilized enough strength to impose its policy of forceful requisition for a while, the peasants always had the defense of ceasing to produce. The Bolsheviks were simply not strong enough to win in a frontal attack on the peasants. It was this situation which convinced Lenin in 1921 that the Party must beat a strategic retreat and the NEP, with its more liberal policy toward the peasants, must be introduced. The essential thing was to get the economy operating again and this meant above all the restoration of agricultural production. The only possible way to do this was by restoration of the peasant capitalist as the motive force and the market system as the regulator. By restoring a money economy — limiting the arbitrary exactions from the peasant and permitting him to sell his grain in the open market and to buy what he could from the urban economy through a trade system restored to private hands — the NEP would encourage the growth of food supplies and of agricultural raw materials on the one hand and would encourage the restoration of industry on the other. These two halves of the economy would be joined to each other by a restoration of private trade. Each half would find a market and a source of supply in the other. Moreover, the growth of agricultural output would again make possible some exports to the world market which would give the Soviet Union foreign exchange with which to buy equipment and raw materials essential for getting industry back into operation.

The NEP was a great success, which is not hard to understand. The recovery from War Communism was essentially a problem of putting existing production capacity back into operation. The peasants had to be persuaded to go out into the fields again and get the ground plowed and planted. In industry it was a matter of drawing the workers back into the cities and the factories, of getting machinery repaired and rolling again. Of course it was not as simple as it sounds. All of these restorations depended on one other. For the process to start there must be fuel for the factories, there must be some seed and draft animals. It was impossible for the rudimentary planning apparatus then in existence to do anything with this problem but it is the sort of problem that the market system handles superbly. Given a free hand, capitalists and traders mediate between supplies and demands with great flexibility. And as long as they are not afraid of government expropriation they work hard at it. There was indeed rapid restoration of the economy during the NEP period. Industrial output had in 1921 fallen to less than a fifth of the prewar level but by 1926 it had regained the lost ground. Similarly, in agriculture, at the beginning of the NEP, the total area planted to crops had fallen by more than a third from the prewar level and output had declined even more — to less than half the prewar level. But four years later, by 1925, agriculture had recovered the prewar levels, both in terms of output and sown area.

As the prewar level of production was reached, the Party's problem came less and less to be whether it could avoid economic collapse and could retain control of the country. The emphasis now shifted to the question of what path of economic policy it should mark out for itself.

The Rightists' answer to the question was essentially that the policy of the NEP could simply be extended more or less indefinitely in the future. They argued that it would be compatible with further growth, even when the economy had been completely restored to the prewar levels of output. They recognized that the economic problem would then take on a new dimension, one of adding new capacity. That is, to keep the process of growth going, it would be necessary to make new investments, rather than simply putting existing capacity back into operation. The Rightists thought that funds for the necessary investment would be obtainable via the following kind of mechanism. As output of industry grew, there would be provided a flow of goods which could be exchanged with the peasantry for additional agricultural produce which would in turn provide raw materials for the growing industry and food for the growing industrial labor force. The peasantry, protected from arbitrariness in requisitions and more or less unmolested by the government, would gladly produce this surplus. As this process continued, industry would reduce its costs and this would mean profits that could be plowed back into industrial expansion. As the peasants prospered, they would begin to generate a stream of savings which the state could borrow or otherwise tap to augment the profits of industry for investment in expansion of industry. The process could not be forced but it was one that would work and one that would not threaten the political stability of the regime.

Thus one of the important themes of the Rightist position was the emphasis on agriculture. Expansion and improvement in the efficiency of agriculture were given great emphasis as prerequisites for the industrialization program. A prosperous agriculture was necessary to insure an adequate flow of raw materials and food to the expanding industrial sector and also to provide a market for industry as it expanded. If industry was to grow there had to be a market for the output and it was the increasingly prosperous peasantry that would provide such a market. This is only the skeleton of the argument; all of the main points were backed up in detail with additional arguments. But the best way to get a fuller appreciation of the thinking of the Rightists of the party is to contrast it with the arguments of their opponents. Let us now turn to the position of the other side.

The Leftist Position. During most of the NEP period there were opposition groups within the Party which disagreed in various ways with the ideas and policies of the Rightists who, as we have said, were responsible for government policy. One strain of opposition was constituted by the Leftists, whose principal figures were Trotsky, Zinov'ev, and Kamenev. But the theoretical basis of their arguments was largely the work of the economist Evgenii Preobrazhenskii. The Leftists' views on the route which industrialization should follow were quite different from those of the Rightists.

The opposition found flaws in the reasoning of the Rightists, flaws which they thought would doom their proposed policies for industrialization. They argued that policies which had admittedly been successful in accomplishing the restoration work of the NEP would not work as a method of further industrialization once industry was completely restored. One half of their argument concerned the investment requirements of industrialization. They insisted that the investment requirements were far greater than the Rightists realized. The amounts of accumulation that would be required for further industrialization greatly exceeded those that had been needed during the restoration period. In support of this emphasis on the problem of accumulation the opposition advanced a number of arguments.

1. During the NEP years, it had been possible to have big increases in output from relatively small amounts of investment because the investment was mostly for repair and restoration. The problem had been simply to patch up a capital stock that was already of considerable size. This would not be true in the future.

2. The situation in the late twenties was such that in actuality the Soviet economy was eating into its capital — fixed assets were

wearing out faster than new investment took their place. This process could not continue indefinitely; the country would have to pay later for the capital-consumption binge it was on.

3. Much emphasis was given to the idea that industrialization would call for investment throughout all branches of the economy. There would have to be investment on a broad front to get the economy over the hump and started on the path of rapid economic growth. For instance, there would have to be investment in transportation to move the increased volume of output. There would have to be investment in the cities to provide housing, schools, and medical care for the growing industrial labor force. (This, incidentally, is a point that is strongly supported by the experience of countries that are planning for development today.)

4. Closely associated with this argument was the idea that if industrialization were to be completely successful, the planners would have to use the latest developments in technology. For instance, electricity would have to be used to provide the motive power for industry; very large, specialized plants would have to be built and equipped with the most modern machinery. If the planners tried to patch up and extend the present ways of doing things, industry would remain backward, inefficient, unproductive. Successful industrialization policy would require that industry be reconstructed on a modern level. But all these measures for making industry very productive were highly "capital-intensive." That is, they would require the investment of relatively large amounts of rubles to raise industrial output by one ruble's worth.

5. Another point was made (a variation of the one above) that in general the branches of industry which produce steel, machinery, and other commodities required to carry out an investment program are in any case quite capital-intensive in comparison with the branches of industry which produce consumer goods. To build the blast furnaces to produce the steel to make the machines to make other machines which would ultimately make consumer goods is a long, drawn-out process. In short, Preobrazhenskii explained very eloquently all the reasons why industrialization inevitably requires that labor and other resources be tied up for a long period of time before they finally produce

something that people can put in their mouths or on their backs.

The other half of the Leftists' argument had to do with the possibilities of financing these investments. They were skeptical about being able to drain off from a thriving agricultural sector enough resources to finance these heavy requirements. It was true that in the period before the revolution the peasantry had provided large amounts of resources or funds for the financing of the industrialization that had begun under the tsarist regime. But these contributions had been achieved only by a peculiar system. The tsarist regime had collected large monetary payments from the peasants in the form of taxes and in the form of "redemption payments," i.e., the payments on the loans which the government had advanced the peasants when it abolished serfdom and settled land on them. So the peasants were forced to sell their grain to get money, even when they had not had an adequate supply to feed themselves. The grain thus poured on the market was cheap enough so that large amounts of it could be sold abroad in the world market. These exports gave Russia a foreign trade surplus which enabled the Russian government to accumulate gold and go on the gold standard and to pay interest on foreign debt. These two measures (i.e., the gold standard and a foreign trade surplus) provided in turn the kind of security that attracted foreign investors to put money into Russian industry and to lend funds to the Russian government. The regime then spent these funds for direct investments in industrialization and as subsidies to encourage private investment in industry. Thus the tsarist regime had worked out an effective scheme for putting much of the burden of industrialization on the peasantry.

But the Leftists argued that since they were now freed of the compulsion of this system, the peasants would never provide the resources for industrialization. They would in effect eat up the grain that had previously gone through this roundabout route to build new factories. Or if the government tried to get the grain away from the peasants by exchanging large amounts of industrial goods for it, this would aggravate the shortage of goods and make the urban worker unhappy. The peasants would never voluntarily part with that much grain — nor would they make any money savings which the government could borrow to finance industrialization. Stated briefly, the position of the Leftists was that industrialization would require tremendous savings and that these would have to come mostly from the peasantry, but that the peasants would never voluntarily make this sacrifice if the government continued to follow a policy of encouraging peasant agriculture.

Now each side could find vulnerable points in the arguments of the other. The Rightists tried to argue that the big capital needs which the Leftists emphasized so heavily could be partially avoided by exporting grain to the capitalist world in exchange for machinery and equipment. In other words they could let the capitalist part of the world worry about accumulating the capital required to build factories to build the machinery. This approach would short-circuit the process of capital accumulation and so obviate some of the need for investment.

They also argued that if the Leftist policy were followed, the new industry would suffer a crisis of overproduction. If income were taken away from the peasants to finance the investments needed for industrialization, the peasants would not be able to buy the enlarged output of industry. There is a certain inconsistency in this argument since if the increased output were to consist of investment goods, then there would be nothing to sell the peasants anyway. But in the context of Russian experience it was a natural objection to make. The inadequacy of the domestic market to absorb big increases in output had traditionally been an obstacle to industrialization in Russia.

But the most persistent and effective point in the argument of the Rightists was that the policy of the superindustrializers, as the Leftists were sometimes called, was dangerously adventurist. If their vision of the process of industrialization were to be translated into action, it would destroy that alliance with the peasantry on which the NEP was based. Lenin's analysis of the peasant problem, though made in the dark days of 1921, was still relevant. It was still necessary for the survival of the regime to avoid alienating the peasants in this predominantly agricultural country. If the peasants were now squeezed too hard to finance industrialization, they would again employ the devices of revolt and noncooperation which they had engaged in at the time of the civil war. If this happened, there was a danger that socialism in Russia would be finished. Actually it was on the basis of this issue that Stalin in cooperation with the Rightist group was ultimately able to destroy the power of the left opposition within the Party and to purge the Leftists from the Party.

The Leftists had counterarguments on many of these issues too. The really crucial question, as we have seen, was the relationship with the peasants and here the position of the Leftists was that the policy of encouraging agriculture would result in the growth of power of the most capitalist elements in the countryside. The Soviet peasants were not all alike with respect to their political allegiance and economic characteristics. It was customary to classify them as poor, middle, and rich peasants, depending on how much land they farmed, whether or not they owned equipment and horses, and whether they hired labor or worked for other peasants. The conditions of the NEP encouraged this differentiation. The more ambitious, able, and thrifty, or, from another point of view, the shrewdest and most ruthless, expanded their land holdings, their share of total output, and their power over the other peasants. They also accounted for an increasing share of the grain that was put on the market. The poorer peasants with smaller holdings tended to eat most of what they produced. The richer peasants, or *kulaks,* as they were called, were uncompromisingly capitalistic in their orientation. The Leftists argued that if the official line toward agriculture were continued, the *kulaks* would be in a position to strike against the regime. They would do this by means of withholding grain, the supply of which was coming more and more under their control. Toward the end of the twenties this argument of the Leftists was given added force by the course of events. During 1928 the grain deliveries fell alarmingly from previous levels as *kulaks* withheld grain. (By this time, unfortunately, the Leftists had already been purged from the Party and were unable to exploit this concrete evidence in support of their position.)

Who Was Right? What were the conclusions of this debate? Had the argument shown what the proper policy for industrialization should be? On the theoretical level it looked as if both sides in the debate had more or less proved that the program of the other would never work. Thus the end result of the argument was essentially to pose clearly all the contradictory aspects of the industrialization problem and to demonstrate clearly the nature of the dilemma the regime faced. The Rightists had shown the reasons why the regime must go slowly in its industrialization program; the Leftists had shown the absolute necessity of proceeding very rapidly. It was not that one side was right and the other wrong in its analysis but that the situation they were analyzing itself posed a contradiction. Each side in the debate had painstakingly illuminated one horn of the dilemma the regime found itself in.

As one looks back on this debate from the vantage point of today, it seems to foreshadow the experience of later entrants in the industrialization race. Many other underdeveloped countries are today debating the courses they should follow in trying to industrialize and all of them find that in one way or another they face the same dilemma the Russians faced at the end of the twenties. The intractability of this problem for the planners of countries now seeking to industrialize underscores the seriousness of the difficulties the Russians faced if they really wanted to industrialize and helps explain the willingness of some to look for radical solutions.

As we know, Soviet industrialization was not just a subject for theoretical debate. Despite the theoretical demonstration by these two groups that industrialization must founder on one or the other obstacle, a way was found out of the impasse. The Soviet Union did launch and carry out an ambitious and successful industrialization program. How did this happen? What was missing in the arguments of the two sides in the industrialization debate?

Stalin's Way Out

To understand this part of the story one must turn from the thinkers to the doers and in this period the main doer was Stalin. Although Stalin had used the debate over these issues as a device for destroying his enemies and entrenching himself in control of the Party, he had not really contributed much to the theoretical analysis of the problems of industrialization. But at the point when the two halves of the problem really seemed to be closing in on the Soviet regime, he made his big contribution by organizing a way of escaping the dilemma. His answer to the problem of the crucial relationship with the peasant was collectivization — a rad-

ical change in the institutional setting within which the problem
was to be handled. He more or less evaded the horns of the
dilemma by pushing forward the collectivization of agriculture and
so putting the peasant in a situation where he could not fight back.
On this issue as always it was Stalin's practice to speak from
both sides of his mouth and his statements on the purpose and
rationale of the collectivization are somewhat vague. In retrospect
it seems fairly certain that he made a decision to put the peasants
in collective farms where it would be much easier to force on them
the sacrifice required by industrialization. In the collective farms
the decisions about the division of agricultural output into consumption and transfers to the urban economy would no longer
rest with the individual peasant but would instead be under the
control of representatives of the regime. And the consolidation
of millions of peasant households into a much smaller number of
collective farms would make the problem of control much simpler.

Collective farms had always been regarded as desirable and
were considered the eventual form which agriculture would have
to take in a country of socialism. There had been some experimental beginnings in introducing collective farms as a "socialist"
way of organizing agriculture. But the opinion generally held
was that collectives would only gradually come into being and
that they would take over ultimately as a result of a process of
competition. The peasants would join collective farms voluntarily
when it was demonstrated to them that this was really a superior
framework within which they could carry on their agricultural
endeavors. Much was said, by Stalin as well as by others, about
the technical efficiency of large-scale collective farms. It was hoped
that they would be so much more productive than individual peasant farming that there would be enough output to increase the
amount going to the state and to increase as well the amount left
for the peasants to consume. Part of the reason for the hesitation
about pushing the organization of collective farms was the awareness that a large investment would be required to make them
efficient. The addition of this investment demand on top of the
investment requirements for industry would aggravate the problems of capital accumulation and the planners were eager to avoid
this burden if possible. So at the end of the twenties most influential

opinion and official actions seemed to indicate that agriculture would be collectivized only slowly.

By 1928 it looked as though Stalin had adopted ideas from both sides of the argument. He had called for the establishment of a very ambitious industrialization program in the First Five-Year Plan. As the planners worked out successive drafts of the plan, he demanded higher and higher goals. Planners who insisted that further upward revisions in the goals of the plan were unrealistic were purged and replaced by more pliant types. When the First Five-Year Plan was finally adopted in the spring of 1929 it was a superindustrialization plan that went far beyond what even Preobrazhenskii would have thought feasible. Its goals for investment and growth in the nonagricultural labor force indicated that the peasants would have to bear great sacrifices. But at the same time Stalin was essentially following the NEP approach to the question of relations with the peasants. The First Five-Year Plan set very modest goals for the collectivization of agriculture. It was stated in the First Five-Year Plan that "in the course of these five years, individual peasant farming will play the principal part in the production of agricultural commodities," and this decision was embodied by projecting that state and collective farms would increase their share of the sown acreage from only 2 per cent in 1926–27 to 13.4 per cent in 1932–33. Thus the plan appeared to envisage a policy toward the peasantry which was not much different from the general line of the Party in the NEP period.

When the inconsistency between these two aspects of the plan — the inconsistency which the Leftists had emphasized so strongly in their arguments — began to appear in 1928, Stalin shifted his position and brought the Party along with him in the decision to risk an all-out war with the peasants.

From the fall of 1928 on, grain collections proceeded very unsatisfactorily, amounting to much less than in previous years. It appeared as if the peasants were attempting to say *nyet* to the sacrifice the industrial planners wanted them to make. So the time had come to face up to and find some way of dealing with the dilemma which had been so carefully explored in the industrialization debate. In 1929 Stalin ceased talking about the virtues of voluntary cooperation in collectivizing agriculture and about the technical efficiency of collectives and instituted instead a drive to force the peasants into collectives so that the supplies required for industrialization could be extracted efficiently. This was to be a war which would destroy once and for all the peasantry's ability to interfere with industrialization.

Despite the original modest goals for collectivization which had been established in the First Five-Year Plan, there was begun in 1929 a program to collectivize agriculture completely. In the fall and winter of 1929–30 the drive was greatly intensified and the number of peasant households in the collectives rose from about one million on June 1, 1929, to a little over 14 million on March 1, 1930. This war with the peasants was not won easily. It was accomplished by the devices of terror and repression. Trusted Communists from the cities were mobilized to carry on the work. The army and secret police were used, class hatreds within the village were played on in order to enlist some of the peasants on the side of the regime. The peasants were forced into collective farms willy-nilly; those who opposed the collectives were killed or deported. Altogether some 5 million persons were deported or shot. Collectivization was the most intensive experiment in repression and terror that the regime had ever engaged in up to that point.

Naturally, this frontal attack created havoc in agriculture. The peasants fought back with large-scale destruction of agricultural capital; they burned buildings, slaughtered their livestock, ate up whatever grain supplies were on hand. As the process unfolded it began to look as if the predictions of the Rightists about the dangers of pressing too hard on the peasantry were about to come true. But despite their adverse effects on productivity and efficiency, the collective farms were an extremely efficient device for forcing the peasants to hand over output to the regime. The grain was obtained even though the peasants who had produced it might subsequently starve. Thus in the end Stalin's collectivization program worked and made possible a flow of food and agricultural raw materials to permit the drive toward the goals of the First Five-Year Plan to continue.

This approach of ruthlessly remodeling any institutions that stood in the way of economic growth was paralleled in the treatment of the labor unions and in the attitude toward wages. For a while after the revolution Soviet labor unions had some real power and performed some real functions as devices for expressing and implementing the views of the workers on economic life. At an early stage they gave the workers some voice in the management of enterprises, though this phase was short-lived. Under the New Economic Policy they still retained some vitality and some power to express the workers' feelings and to defend them against the policies of industrial management. The leaders of the unions were permitted to serve in the role of spokesmen for the workers' point of view in the inner councils of the Party and so were able to exert some influence at the highest levels of economic policy. But the continued existence of any autonomy in the unions posed certain threats to industrialization. The workers generally favored an egalitarian approach in wage policy, which interfered with motivation and productivity, and were always asking for increases in wages and consumption. Indeed during much of the NEP period, workers had managed through the unions to obtain wage increases that were larger than productivity increases. Moreover, the union leaders in the Party had generally favored gradualist policies in the industrialization debate. When the industrialization drive began in earnest, it was thought necessary to eliminate even the limited authority and power which the unions still had. They were purged of their leadership and thus lost any ability to defend the workers' point of view at the highest level. The unions were not actually abolished but were placed firmly under Stalin's control. They retained certain neutral administrative responsibilities, such as administration of the social insurance program, but were essentially transformed into another of those Soviet "transmission belts," like the Soviet press, whose function is to pass down to the masses decisions made at the top by the Party.

Economic Growth a Basic Obsession

In this brief narrative we have sketched in only the barest outline of the process that culminated in the First Five-Year Plan and in the collectivization of agriculture. The story is really much more complex than there is space here to describe. For more details on this crucial period in the formation of the Soviet economic system the reader should consult some of the works discussed in the bibliography at the end of the book. The main objective of the summary presented here has been to demonstrate the implacable determination of the Bolshevik regime to force the pace of Soviet economic growth to the utmost and to point out the early date at which this decision was made. The long discussion in the twenties made it clear to the Soviet leaders that it was necessary for them to industrialize rapidly, that this would involve considerable sacrifice, and that it would thus require the use of strong pressure on the population by the regime to effect it. It was in the name of industrialization that the totalitarian terror machine was perfected. This was the purpose which justified the killing or deportation of 5 million peasants and the destruction of the power of the labor unions. In a larger sense the imperative of rapid industrialization was made the justification for the imposition of complete totalitarian dictatorship on the population of the country and it was even part of the rationale for remodeling the Party itself along more totalitarian and monolithic lines. To enforce the decision to industrialize and to remove the possibility of arguing about it or pointing out the sacrifices involved when the questions began to appear, opposition groups were purged from the Party and the toleration of different viewpoints or of open discussion, even within the Party, was prohibited.

This obsession with the need for rapid growth has not diminished over the years. Stalin spent a great deal of his later life trying to justify the industrialization decision with all its sacrifices and insisting that the process must continue. The aim of rapid growth has been institutionalized in the slogan "to overtake and surpass the capitalistic countries." This is a cliché which the reader of Soviet propaganda, of the speeches of Soviet leaders, and even of the serious economic literature of the Soviet Union finds ever present. And it has been thrown at the Soviet citizen until it is as immutable a part of his environment as the rising and setting of the sun. Undoubtedly some Soviet citizens resent this goal that the regime has chosen for them, but at the same time many identify themselves with it and consider it a legitimate objective for their society. The Soviet leaders, and to a considerable extent the Soviet population, see themselves engaged in a heroic struggle to overcome economic backwardness and catch up with the capitalist countries in the shortest possible time.

Current doctrine, as expressed in the program of the Communist Party adopted at the 22nd Party Congress, proclaims that the principal economic task of the next decade or so is to complete the building of the material-technical basis of communism and to create the era of abundance that will usher in the communist millennium. Characteristically, these great events are to coincide with surpassing the United States in per capita output.

In trying to understand "what kind of thing the Soviet economy is," therefore, and in trying to assess how it works and what it can accomplish, one should never forget that the objective of rapid economic growth is a goal which the Party leadership set for the Russians thirty-five years ago and that this has been their primary obsession ever since.

3

Soviet Planning

The set of economic institutions which the Soviet leaders have created to accomplish their goal of rapid growth and to enforce their views on priorities regarding resource use has been labeled with many different terms — socialism, planning, state capitalism, the command economy. Each of these epithets emphasizes some essential feature of the system, though none of them are well enough defined to convey very fully just what is essential and distinctive about the Soviet system. The goal of this chapter and of the two following ones is to give an integral view of how the Soviet economic system operates — by making these terms more concrete and by showing how the connotations of each fit into the general picture.

The economic problem of any society is to use efficiently the resources available to it to accomplish whatever goals may be established for the society. (We will ignore for the moment the issue of how the goals are decided on and who has a part in their determination.) The economist describes this problem as the problem of economic efficiency or the rational allocation of resources. The totality of things which the individuals of a society would like to see accomplished far outruns what is feasible with the resources at hand. Hence choices must be made about priorities and an effort made to see that resources are used in such a way that they make the greatest possible contribution toward the achievement of the desired objectives. It will be useful in thinking about the Soviet economy to recognize two sub-problems implicit in this general problem: (1) the problem of coordinating the activities of the different participants in the social process of production and (2) the problem of optimizing (that is, making rational choices among) alternatives.

Coordination involves the achievement of internal consistency among the actions of producers and consumers and of others whose actions are interdependent. The output of coal must be great enough to supply the needs of all those who require coal for producing their output, such as steel or electric power, or there will not be enough steel and electric power. On the other hand, to produce more coal than is needed would be a waste of resources. The output of automobiles and clothing must be in proportions consistent with people's preferences or there will be an excess of one and a shortage of the other. If it is desired that a certain share of the national income be invested, it is necessary that among the many things produced by the economy there be investment goods, such as cement and machinery, in the required proportions. However, the achievement of internal consistency, the balancing of supply and demand, is not enough to ensure economic efficiency. It is also necessary that everything be produced in the most efficient way. For instance, to satisfy the demand for fuel by producing enough coal is not in itself sensible if the fuel needs of the economy could be met at a lower cost, or with a smaller input of resources, by producing fuel oil and natural gas instead of coal. Throughout the economy the objective is to have producers follow courses of action which use the smallest possible input of resources to meet the required level of output. For an economic system to be rational, it must meet both these objectives more or less adequately. It must provide the information and the motivation that will induce those who make decisions about production and about resource use to satisfy these conditions.

In a market economy such as that of the United States the achievement of the two aspects of economizing depends on the operation of markets, the price system, and profit maximization. Through the operation of supply and demand, the prices of things which are badly wanted or are in short supply move upward; the prices of things which are available in excess or which people no longer want so much are pushed downward. This is true for everything that is bought and sold, including the inputs used in producing goods, such as labor, materials, and capital, as well as the finished goods that are sold to ultimate consumers. Producers, whose aim is to make as much profit as they can, adjust their plans in accordance with these price movements. If the price of a given commodity increases, that encourages the production and discourages the consumption of that commodity — and conversely, lower prices encourage use and discourage production. This mechanism works flexibly in our economy to eliminate shortages and over-supplies and to direct resources into the production of what is wanted most.

The price system also aids in achieving the second element of rationality, namely, efficiency. Profits depend not only on producing the right things but also on producing them as cheaply as possible. In trying to cut costs, businessmen are guided by prices. In deciding whether to use one material or another, in choosing the best location for a plant, in selecting one production process over another, or in calculating to what extent they should substitute more machinery for labor, they consider the prices they will have to pay for inputs in order to see what the comparative costs of alternatives will be. The prices on the inputs bought by producers in running their businesses, just as the prices on the outputs they sell, can be thought of as a measure of how valuable these goods are in the overall estimation of society, taking into account how scarce they are, how much it costs to produce them, and how productive they are. In trying to cut costs to increase profits, businessmen are at the same time minimizing the cost to society of producing their output. The mechanisms of supply and demand and profit maximization do not work perfectly but they are constantly pushing our economy in the direction of the optimum use of our resources.

In the Soviet economy, economic decision making has traditionally been guided by a set of rules and pressures that relies only secondarily on profit calculations, a price system, or markets. This decision-making process is the essence of what distinguishes the Soviet-type economy from the market economy. In the Soviet economy most property belongs to the government and most economic decision making is in the hands of hired manager-bureaucrats. Markets operating according to the laws of supply and demand have been the exception rather than the rule and managers have made their decisions not in accordance with profit maximizing considerations but on the basis of other criteria.

Beginning in the early nineteen sixties, some Russians, of whom E. G. Liberman is the best known, recommended reforms in Soviet economic administration that would put more emphasis on markets, prices, and profit considerations. Some experimental moves in this direction were first made in 1964 and 1965 when a considerable number of enterprises in the consumer goods industries were allowed to decide for themselves many details which had formerly been determined from above — details such as the assortment of goods to be produced. In addition, profit was made the most important measure for evaluating success and enterprise management was given a strong motivation to maximize profits by tying management's bonus system to profit performance. In 1965 Liberman-style reform was extended to all industrial enterprises, though not in as radical a form as Liberman had recommended. These changes represent a significant inroad on the traditional principles of Soviet economic organization and it is quite likely that as time goes on the Soviet economy will shed more and more those distinctive differences from the market economy which we have described above. But it has not traveled very far along this road yet and, for the present, Soviet enterprise management still operates in an environment where the constraints on its right to make various kinds of economic decisions are so serious, and the incentives to which it is subject are so unusual, that it is quite wrong to assert, as is sometimes done, that the Russians seem to be abandoning planning in favor of the profit motive and market methods of control. This point will be developed more fully in Chapter 5 when we describe more concretely what the Liberman-style reforms are, Soviet experience with them so far, and how they fall short of the market model.

To understand how the Soviet economy operates, then, means essentially to understand how economic decisions are made in this environment and to ask whether the Soviet economy is efficient is to ask whether these decisions are made rationally. In thinking about this problem, it is helpful to realize that decisions about resource use in the U.S.S.R. are made in a number of more or less distinct spheres, differentiated from each other by the fact that different people are involved, that different mechanisms operate, and that the criteria and incentives which guide decision making in each are different.

Decision Making in the Soviet Economy

1. One sphere of decision making has to do with the setting of general goals by the leadership. This sphere involves such questions as the desired rate of growth, the allocation of the gross national product between consumption and investment, "strategic" decisions about what areas of potential technological change to concentrate on. To a large extent these are questions of ends rather than of means and can only be answered by appeal to ideological and political rather than economic considerations. There is an important issue here as to whether the leaders have goals and preferences which diverge from those of the population. Many socialist thinkers have postulated that planners should be subject to consumers' sovereignty, i.e., that they should take the preferences of the population as to the composition of the output of the economy as a point of departure in drawing up their plans. But this is an unrealistic assumption for the Soviet type of socialism. The Soviet leaders have created the system of central planning for the express purpose of imposing on the population the policy of sacrificing current consumption to achieve growth which we have described above, a policy which the Russian people probably would not themselves choose if they had any control over the matter. One might argue about the propriety of the leaders arrogating to themselves decisions about goals but the dominance of planners' preferences over those of the population is a fact of the Soviet system which will be taken for granted in the discussion which follows.

The most interesting thing about this sphere of decision making is that in practice the distinction between ends and means, which ought to be observed here, has often been blurred. The powers-that-be at the top of the Soviet decision-making hierarchy very often confuse ends and means and then tell planners how they should settle some issue, such as what size to build plants or where to grow what crops, rather than simply stating what the ultimate priorities are. In doing so, the powers-that-be often impose on the planners their own irrational prejudices and so frustrate the achievement by the planners of a set of decisions that would maximally further the ends of the leadership. For example, Stalin always pushed the growth of the steel industry in accordance with the syllogism that (1) it is desired to maximize the rate of growth of the economy; (2) the best way to get growth in the economy as a whole is to expand the steel industry; (3) hence it is desirable to maximize the growth of steel output. Any economist could have told him that the minor premise is wrong and that a reduction in the rate of growth of the steel industry might well have been a better way to maximize the growth of the economy as a whole. Another example is the traditional insistence the leaders have always put on the proposition that to maximize growth, the plan should show the "means of production" as growing much faster than the "means of consumption." This is a Marxist prejudice that does not in fact guarantee the fastest possible growth of the economy.

2. The most visible and obvious sphere of decision making in Soviet resource allocation, and the part of the planning process which absorbs most of the energies of Soviet planners, is the construction of the annual plans. The main preoccupation of the people engaged in this part of planning is to achieve balance between the supply and demand of all the important commodities in the economy. The difficulty of accomplishing this and the procedures by which it is done in the U.S.S.R. will be the principal topic for discussion in this chapter, to be taken up in a moment. Let us only emphasize here that construction of the annual plan does represent one aspect of decision making and also of resource allocation in that it fixes the level of output of various commodities and allocates output among potential users for the current year. Because the element of coordination in this process is just in itself so complex and, in the absence of a market, requires so much effort, the people who carry it out can afford little attention to problems of optimizing. On investigating what considerations dominate the outcome, it turns out that decisions are as likely to be determined by bureaucratic bargaining strength as by ob-

jective economic criteria. This sphere is differentiated from others also by its time horizon and its periodicity — it is done on an annual basis.

3. A third class of decisions we will call "design decision making." Some examples are the choice of a location for factories; deciding whether electricity is to be produced by steam or by hydroelectric generating plants; determining to what extent the railroads are to operate with diesel, steam, or electric locomotives. The engineers responsible for designing tractors must decide whether they are going to specify gasoline or diesel engines. The hallmark of this class of decisions is that, although they are more or less divorced from issues of current allocation, once they are made they foreclose alternatives and narrow the range of choice about resource use for a considerable time into the future. Once a plant has been located in a certain place, this then implies certain amounts of transportation to move the raw materials to it and to move products to market as the plant operates in years to come. Once it has been decided to equip tractors with one type of engine, this fixes the proportions between diesel fuel and gasoline required in the output of the refining industry in future years. These decisions in the Soviet economy are generally not made by the managers of production enterprises but by a special class of engineers and economists working in distinct organizations called project-making organizations. These are generally located above the level of the enterprise in the organizational structure and the planners who work in them are controlled by a distinct set of rules and incentives. Rather than responding to the set of performance indicators that influence the managers of production enterprises, project makers refer their decisions to economic theory and to more abstract criteria of rationality and "effectiveness." In making a decision about the location of some plant, they would not be influenced by a bonus for the performance of the plant but by more theoretical ideas about what constitutes a rational policy of location.

4. There is an extremely important class of decisions concerned with fulfillment on a day-to-day basis and at lower administrative levels of the decisions made in other spheres. The job of decision making is not really complete when the national economic

plan has been drawn up and approved. It must still be executed and the job of execution is in the hands of a group of officials who are nominally subordinate to other decision makers but who in fact have decision-making power over the final outcome. The plan will not be fulfilled exactly — because it is an imperfect plan, because people who are in charge of fulfilling it can change it, because some flaws and emergencies will have to be coped with as they arise. Some parts of the plan will be overfulfilled, others will be underfulfilled. Some decisions promulgated by higher levels will indeed be carried out, some will be ignored, others will be changed in execution. The assortment of output specified in the plan for a factory may be violated and performance may fall short of plan both in terms of quality and quantity. What the plan "commands" in the way of inventory investment may not be obeyed and orders for innovation may not be heeded. This is what the Russians talk about as the problem of plan execution or plan fulfillment. It will be discussed at length in the chapter following this one.

5. Finally, it is useful to distinguish an area of decision making about resource allocation involving the relations of the Soviet regime with households. Quantitatively, the most important resource in any economy is labor. In operating its production establishment, the Soviet regime must procure labor services from the Soviet population and allocate them among different occupations, regions, and industries. On the other hand, it must distribute among laborers whatever share of the national income it is setting aside for the maintenance of the population. The goal of efficiency here, of course, is to coordinate these two allocations so as to maximize the productive effort and talent which the regime can extract from the population for a given commitment of resources to consumption. In this area of the Soviet economy, the mechanisms of resource allocation resemble fairly closely those of the market economy and there is considerable dependence on market principles. Despite the practical necessity of relying to a large degree on the mechanism of supply and demand in this sphere of decision making, however, the planners have never quite understood the requirements of the market principle and some interesting problems in this area will be taken up in Chapter 7.

Balancing Supply and Demand in the Annual Plan

It is difficult to appreciate the complexity of the problem of co-ordination involved in a modern industrial economy. The intricacy of the interrelationships among different economic magnitudes staggers the imagination. The basic insight on which the science of economics is based is that almost all economic magnitudes depend on all other economic magnitudes. The number of automobiles that can be sold, for instance, depends on the price of automobiles relative to other goods and on the incomes of people. Each of these in turn depends upon other factors which are in their turn the result of other interrelationships and so on ad infinitum. Similarly, if one asks how much steel should be produced, the answer is seen to depend on how much is to be produced of all the steel-using products and each of these magnitudes is in turn a function of many others.

Input-Output Relationships. A good way to gain an appreciation of the kind of interrelationships that make practical planning so difficult is to look at the picture of an economy provided by an "input-output table." An input-output table is a sort of short-hand statistical description of an economy, organized in a special way. A highly schematic and oversimplified example is shown in Table 3.1. This table will merit some unhurried study. Some experimentation with it will help greatly in understanding the mutual interdependence among different parts of an economic system. Looking across any of the rows of this table, one can see the distribution of the output of any given industry among its various users. For instance, the first row shows that of the total output of 412.4 billion kilowatt-hours of electric power produced during the year in this hypothetical economy, 24.7 billion kilowatt-hours was used by the electric power industry for its own needs; 21.0 billion kilowatt-hours went to the coal industry; 29.9 billion kilowatt-hours was used by producers of oil and gas; various amounts went to other branches of industry, to agriculture, and to transport. Finally some was left over for meeting the needs of households and other "final" consumers. Similarly, in each of the other rows, the disposition of the total output of some branch of the economy is

TABLE 3.1 Input-Output Table

Unit of Measurement	Producing Sector	Electric Power	Coal	Oil and Gas	Iron and Steel	Machinery	Chemicals	Lumber and Wood Products	Construction Materials	Textiles and Apparel	Food Processing	Agriculture	Transport	Other	Households	Government	Investment	Total Output
BKWH	Electric Power	24.7	21.0	29.9	27.9	51.0	29.5	13.7	36.2	24.4	16.8	15.7	30.6	51.5	26.9	1.9	10.7	412.4
MT	Coal	160.7	44.5	.8	123.3	8.1	3.7	3.6	14.8	3.3	8.6	5.6	48.1	75.4	25.8	3.4	2.0	531.7
10MB	Oil and Gas	17.85	.35	35.00	7.14	12.81	9.73	16.73	10.43	1.89	11.34	42.00	54.60	59.01	11.20	10.26	7.00	307.30
$B	Iron and Steel	.02	.04	.02	2.58	3.26	.15	.13	.29	.03	.08	.03	.12	.62	.08	.20	1.60	9.25
$B	Machinery	.03	.10	.05	.28	8.28	.03	.05	.03	.03	.07	.91	.10	.03	1.76	8.15	9.33	29.23
$B	Chemicals	.01	.03	.06	.10	1.19	2.21	.18	.05	.61	.08	.43	.42	.58	.60	1.23	.29	8.07
$B	Lumber and Wood Products	.03	.40	.01	.08	.44	.17	3.12	.06	.14	.36	.12	.17	1.16	2.20	.73	3.01	12.32
$B	Construction Materials	.02	.01	—	.01	.13	.04	.37	1.29	.01	.07	.02	.06	.08	.56	.13	5.67	8.16
$B	Textiles and Apparel	.01	.13	.01	.11	.38	.51	.03	.07	15.37	.01	—	.14	.91	23.68	.92	.57	43.19
$B	Food Processing	.02	—	—	.01	.01	.43	.01	.01	.62	13.37	1.58	—	.85	32.37	8.43	.09	57.82
$B	Agriculture	—	—	—	—	—	.01	.03	.01	4.47	16.47	12.44	.02	.21	18.54	1.49	.01	53.69
10BTM	Transport	—	59.0	26.8	24.7	2.9	4.0	33.9	17.6	1.8	9.8	13.9	.3	2.6	17.2	12.3	3.4	230.2
$B	Other	.23	.25	.46	.30	1.04	.81	.43	.43	.33	.53	.31	.58	.33	1.55	.58	.10	8.26
TMY	Labor	405	1,254	191	990	6,915	754	3,210	2,037	3,740	2,530	34,200	6,941	7,324	3,696	13,983	6,302	94,472

BKWH = billion kilowatt-hours
MT = million tons
10MB = ten million barrels
$B = billion dollars
10BTM = ten billion ton-miles
TMY = thousand man-years

shown. The bottom row of the table, below the heavy line, shows the distribution of the labor force of the economy among the various sectors. During the year a total of 94,472 thousand man years were worked and of this total 405 thousand were for the electric power industry, 1,254 thousand were in the coal industry, 191 thousand in the production of oil and gas, 990 thousand in the iron and steel industry, and so on across the row.

Looked at in another way, this table shows other important relationships. Glancing down any column, one can see the amounts of various goods and services that each industry bought and used in the process of producing its own output in the course of the year. For instance, in order to produce its 412.4 billion kilowatt-hours of electric power, the electric power industry had to consume 160.7 million tons of coal, oil and gas equivalent to 178.5 million barrels of oil, and the amounts shown of transportation, labor, and other inputs. For each industry the column shows the inputs from all other industries which were required by the given industry for the production of the volume of output it produced. Thus all the numbers to the left of the last four columns and above the "labor" row characterize the mutual interdependence of the demand for the output of any industry with the demand for the output of all other industries. How much coal will be needed depends on the levels of output of all those industries that require coal for their operation.

These interrelationships are more or less stable, at least for relatively short periods of a few years. This is because they are based on certain technological facts. In the case of the electric power industry, for instance, the consumption of 160.7 million tons of coal and 178.5 million barrels of fuel oil to produce 412.4 billion kilowatt-hours of electricity is a reflection of the fact that, with the presently available technology and given the efficiency of the equipment now in use, there is required on the average a certain number of BTU, or calories, to produce one KWH of electric power. (See Chapter 7.) Similarly the input of iron and steel products required to produce the 29.2 billion dollars worth of machinery reflects the existing state of technology in the machinery industry, the kind of things that the machinery industry produces, and so on. Some of these interrelationships are more stable than others and all can change over time as technology changes and with other factors.

By and large, such shifts proceed fairly slowly and the relationships shown in the operation of the economy in a given year can be expected to hold fairly well for the near future.

This table will illustrate very neatly the task of the Soviet planners. A little experimentation shows that the amount of any commodity which the planners should produce depends on how much of everything else is going to be produced. In the table, as we have shown it, everything just matches. Each industry has been able to sell all the output it produced and there is enough left over to meet household, investment, and government demands. But as the planners look forward to the task of drawing up the plan for the next year, obviously there will have to be some changes in output. Let us suppose, for example, that the planners want to increase the output of electric power used by households by 20 billion kilowatt-hours, which is an increase equal to about 5 per cent of the total output of 412.4 billion kilowatt-hours in the year to which the table refers. What will the impact of this single change be on the work of all the sectors of the economy? Clearly there will be some impact on all the different sectors, not just on the electric power industry alone. In order to produce this extra amount of power, the electric power industry will have to consume more coal, more labor, more transportation, and so on. If it took a certain number of tons of coal to produce the 412.4 billion kilowatt-hours in the previous year, it will take about 5 per cent more to increase output by 5 per cent and so on down the line. The electric power industry will require larger inputs from all the industries which supply it and this of course means that the output of every other industry will have to increase. But this is far from the end of the story. If each of the industries which supplies inputs to the electric power industry must increase its output, each will in turn require larger inputs from other industries. Thus there must be another round of adjustments, which will have to be followed by another, and so on in endless repercussion. Moreover, these are the kinds of interrelationships where there are wheels within wheels. For instance, the electric power industry will have to have more coal, but since considerable amounts of electric power are used in coal mining, the coal industry will have to be supplied with more electric power in order to meet the increased demand. So the electric power industry in turn will have to consume still more coal.

This example takes for granted that there is no bottleneck in the capacity of each of these sectors of the economy to produce the output required if it gets enough current inputs. We have assumed that once the planners figure out just how much each industry should produce and insure that there will be available to each industry all the required amounts of power, fuel, and materials, then each industry will be able to produce its assigned output. In fact, however, this may not always be true since the production capacity of the industry, that is, the number of plants it has and the amount of equipment it has for turning out its product, may be inadequate to handle the assigned production program. In such a case it will be necessary to construct new capacity. In the case of the electric power industry, for instance, it may turn out that the assigned output of electric power cannot be produced without construction of new power stations. If this happens, there will be an induced need for more investment, and the amounts of goods available for investment, namely, the amounts shown in the next-to-last column of the input-output table, will have to be increased over whatever initial levels were previously planned. To build this electric power station will require some output from the machinery industry, from the iron and steel industry, from the construction materials industry, etc. This in turn will generate a new chain reaction of demands on all sectors of the economy. Whatever scheme the planners finally arrive at, it must not require more capacity in any industry than is at hand or can be added. The labor supply also sets a limit to total output — a production program that required a labor input for all industries taken together in excess of the labor force would not be feasible.

Or consider the problem posed for the planners by the regime's decisions concerning the military program. Suppose that the government decides that it must provide a bigger defense program than in the previous year in the form of missiles, fissionable material, and an electronic defense network. To carry out this policy would require more output from the corresponding industries, such as machinery and electrical equipment, and would probably also require construction and labor. Now try to trace the impact of this decision on all the sectors of the economy. The increased output of missiles from the machinery industry will require more output from the metal industry, which in turn will create new demands on the output of all the industries that supply inputs to the metals industry. Again from this one decision there will be almost endless ramifications reaching out into all areas of the economy. In the planned economy these interactions do not work themselves out automatically as the mysterious laws of price and of supply and demand go to work, but must be foreseen and taken care of ahead of time by the planners so that the required output will be included in someone's plan — and will be produced and available when required.

Finally, the table also implies some other kinds of equilibria which the planners must consider. All those man-years shown along the bottom row imply wage-earners employed by enterprises who will receive in the aggregate a certain amount of money income. But these laborers are the breadwinners of the households whose consumption is shown in the households column of the table. Obviously these two amounts have to be matched with each other. Suppose that in the previous year these magnitudes were nicely coordinated so that employees were paid the right amount and were taxed the right amount and that the goods sold to households were priced in such a way that the total payments to the workers just enabled them to buy the amount that was made available for them to buy. Suppose that in the next year an increase in total output of the economy is planned which will require additions to the labor force. Or there may be some changes in the average wage level. As a result of such changes, the total money incomes of households will be increased by a certain amount and the planners will have to make some adjustments on the other side to balance this off. They could tax away the increased money incomes; they might plan to produce the same volume of consumer goods as in the previous year but sell them at higher prices; or they might increase the output of consumer goods appropriately, leaving the prices and the tax rates unchanged. If the last is done, there will of course have to be a new round of adjustments in all the planned figures since the production of more consumer goods will require the employment of more labor in those industries, additional inputs from other industries, and so on through the entire cycle once again.

It is obvious that the input-output table shown in Table 3.1 represents a highly oversimplified picture of the interrelationships involved in the economy. In a real economy there are not just thirteen branches but several hundred; moreover, the final claimants on output comprise not only households, investment, and government — there are also exports, increases in inventory, military uses, and others. But even this simplified table illustrates clearly our main point; namely, that it is impossible to plan the activity of any one sector of the economy in isolation from the rest. The decisions of people in charge of planning any one aspect of the economy have an impact on the decisions of people planning the activities of all other sectors of the economy and there must be some mechanism for coordination.

The kind of input-output table shown in Table 3.1 can be recast in a way that makes it possible to express the problem of balance in the form of a mathematical problem, amenable to handling on high-speed computers. But, paradoxically, the input-output approach was developed in the United States rather than in the Soviet Union where it would seem to be so much more useful. Following Stalin's death, when Soviet economists became freer to follow the development of economics in other countries outside the Soviet Bloc, they became intrigued with input-output analysis and have been experimenting intensively with it as an aid to planning. More will be said about these efforts below but first we must discuss how they have tried to cope with the balancing problem in their planning thus far.

The Soviet Mechanisms for Coordination. Construction of the annual plan involves essentially the kind of balancing problem discussed above. The core of the annual plan is a statement of output levels for all outputs and an allocation of these outputs among various consumers, both final and intermediate consumers. At the level of the individual enterprise, the annual plan is essentially a statement of what and how much it is to produce and of how much it will be allotted in the way of inputs for this purpose. These imply many other kinds of targets as well such as labor productivity and norms for material use per unit of output. Also, when the physical amounts for inputs and outputs are multiplied by the corresponding prices, there emerges a financial plan paralleling the physical plan. The annual plan also always contains many comparisons with the previous year. But the skeleton of the

plan is the output assignment and the allocation of inputs to the
enterprise. How do the Soviet planners succeed in setting output
levels and allocating inputs so that supply equals demand for
everything and so that the production assignments to enterprises
are feasible? Our information about the balancing process is not
really very complete. Moreover, the Russians have repeatedly reorganized the planning process over the last fifteen years so that,
just as we think we are getting to understand the assignment of
roles and the sequence of operations, the whole drama is re-
written. The process of annual plan making defies easy description
but the following guidelines will be helpful in understanding its
general operation.

1. *Only the most aggregative kind of coordination is carried on
at the center.* The whole plan is not drawn up in Moscow but
rather the entire hierarchical pyramid of Soviet economic organizations participates in the process. At each level, people operate
with different degrees of detail, subject to varying degrees of constraint. The whole plan is finally produced by a process of negotiation and reconciliation between the different levels.

The process starts at the top with the formulation by the Council of Ministers of very general goals for such economic magnitudes
as the increase in industrial and agricultural output, the level of
new investment, the allocation for military expenditures, the volume
of sales to households, and so forth. These recommendations are
then sent to the central planning bodies. In the last fifteen years
the central planning machinery of the Soviet Union has gone
through many metamorphoses — the agencies have been split up,
recombined, renamed and renamed again, and their responsibilities
redefined on several occasions. At one time, planning responsibilities
were concentrated primarily in the State Planning Commission,
commonly called the Gosplan. After the Second World War there
was a great proliferation of specialized planning agencies to work
on particular aspects of planning, such as Gosstroi for construction
planning, Gossnab for working out input norms, and a succession
of agencies for coordinating scientific research and technical progress. The Gosplan was on several occasions divided into two
specialized bodies, one concerned with long range planning, the
other with annual balancing. In the early sixties the number of
central planning agencies had so increased that a kind of super-

planning organ — the Supreme Council of the National Economy — was established to co-ordinate the work of the co-ordinators. In the planning reforms of 1965, this lush growth of central planning bodies was pruned severely. But one has the feeling that this is a case of the more things change, the more they remain the same. Despite all the redrawing of organization charts and the attaching of new labels to office doors, much of the work must still be done by the same people, across the same desks, on the same forms as before. In what follows, we will speak of this central planning machinery simply as the Gosplan, leaving the reader to consult the sources listed in the suggestions for further reading at the end of the book for more detail on the precise present organization of the central planning bodies and their recent evolution.

Given the aggregate targets from the Council of Ministers, the Gosplan goes through a process of trial-and-error balancing to see what is implied for every sector of the economy. The process of trial and error and successive approximation is manageable at this stage because the Gosplan is working with highly aggregated, and therefore a limited number of, economic magnitudes. In juggling such highly aggregated magnitudes, the Gosplan can resort to rough projections of historical trends; detailed calculations need not be made at this stage. Suppose, for instance, that the instructions from the Council of Ministers call for a 10 per cent increase in industrial output. What are the implications for the industrial labor force? Naturally the economists of the Gosplan do not try to figure out what the increase in labor force in each industrial enterprise will be in order to increase total industrial output by 10 per cent. Rather, they project rough indexes of historical experience. If output per worker has tended to rise in past years at something like 5 per cent, they will assume that output in the year they are planning for can be increased by 5 per cent, with no increase at all in the industrial labor force. The remainder of the planned output increase will have to come from an increase in the labor force. Similarly, the central planners may postulate that this increase in output will require a certain amount of new investment, again on the basis of very aggregative relationships that have held in the past. At this stage, therefore, planning is partly the making of intelligent projections.

A plan in this form, however, would obviously not be an effective instrument for running an economy. To constitute a really operational plan it must be far more specific. The next stage is to pass these aggregative "limits and directives" for output, labor force, materials, investment, etc. down the administrative hierarchy, allocating each of them among sub-units and increasing the amount of detail along the way.

2. *In the process, the central planners concentrate their efforts on key commodities and key sectors.* For instance, a long list of crucial commodities, totaling usually between one and two thousand, is subject to central rationing and allocation. The central planning organs keep even the fairly detailed planning of these commodities under their control. Reconciliation of supply and demand for these materials is effected through what are called "material balances" which are somewhat analogous to the input-output table described earlier. On one side of the ledger are listed all sources of supply such as all the main producers, exports, stockpiles, etc.; on the other, the requirements of all the potential consumers of the item in question are shown. The disposition of other, less critical materials is settled by planning organs at lower levels.

When planning and administration is organized on a branch of industry basis, as before 1957 and since 1965, material balances for minor products of the oil industry, for example, would be under the control of planning groups within the Ministry of the Oil Industry. Between 1957 and 1965, when planning was organized on a territorial basis, an example of a lower level balance might be brick production — production and consumption would be balanced within each region separately, in material balances drawn up by the regional planning agencies. For commodities shipped throughout the Soviet Union the U.S.S.R. Gosplan in these years supervised interregional flows but left it to regional balancers to distribute production assignments and material allocations within the region.

Similarly, the Gosplan is likely to give more attention to the planning of some sectors than of others. It will specify much more detail in its plans for certain branches of industry, such as electric power or machinery, than for others, such as the textile and apparel industries. Many organizations producing consumer goods, such as local industry and producers' cooperatives, are treated only peripherally in the plans drawn up at the center and are left mostly to their own devices in getting the investment funds, labor, and materials required. As another illustration, in investment planning the central planners will consider in detail and require central approval of important projects or those that involve expenditures above certain set limits but will leave the planning and authorization of smaller ones to lower-level officials and planners, subject only to their staying within the totals assigned from above.

3. *The planning process involves constant interaction among various levels of the administrative structure.* The people at the top assign limits and directives to the next lower level of administrative organs; these further disaggregate and allocate these directives and limits among their constituent units, and so on down the line to the point where each enterprise receives a set of limits and directives for output, labor force, investment, materials, supply, and other indicators. At this point, the enterprise is to work out a detailed plan that will be consistent with these overall indicators. But in the process it may find that it cannot meet the output goal with its existing capacity or that it needs more of some input than has been allocated to it. (Or, as the Russians like to picture it, the limits and directives may not fully exhaust the capabilities of the enterprise and so the people in the enterprise may suggest how the plan might be made "harder." But this is more a hortatory myth than an accurate description.)

At this stage there will be arguments and conflicts back and forth between the enterprise and the superior level of administration. Suppose, for instance, that there is a conflict involving the allocation of a certain metal to a machinery plant. The plant management may insist that to produce the assigned output program it needs more of the metal than has been assigned. The administrative agency directly supervising the enterprise (a fuller description of the administrative structure is given in Chapter 4) may counter that if the product is redesigned or if waste and spoilage are cut, the assigned quota will be adequate. If the plant officials can convince their superiors that these are not practical possibilities, then the superior organ may be able to give the plant a bigger allotment of the material by reducing the amount assigned to some other plant within its jurisdiction. If not, it may be necessary to get a larger allocation for the superior organ as a whole and ultimately the planners at the center may have to alter the materials balance for this metal by reducing allocations to other industries or by setting a higher goal for the production of the metal. Such a result will obviously call for the sort of chain reaction described earlier in connection with the input-output table. When such conflicts have been finally worked out, the final version of the aggregative plan is drawn up and ratified at the center and the limits and directives are again passed down the hierarchy and confirmed at each level until each plant receives the final limits and directives from which it is to prepare its final plan. It does so, and when the plan is approved, it constitutes the basis for the work of the enterprise for the coming year.

4. *One of the essential ingredients in this process is that some flexibility be built into the plan.* It is a common practice, for instance, for the superior organs to overstate demands in distributing the limits and directives. An agency responsible for a group of enterprises (such as a "chief administration" in charge of all plants producing electric light bulbs, say) may assign to enterprises in the aggregate 10 per cent more output than its plan actually calls for. Then if some plant does not fulfill its plan, the agency may still meet its goal. Similarly, in the case of wage funds or materials allocations, the chief administration may keep back some of the total allocated to it in order to meet emergencies that arise in the actual course of plan fulfillment. This flexibility makes it possible to handle unforeseen contingencies and to correct some errors that are made in drawing up the plan. Also it is fairly common for plans to be changed in the course of the year and such changes may even be made occasionally in the more aggregative indicators of the central plan. One might argue that these "cushions" constitute a tacit admission that the planning will be inaccurate but, on the other hand, such flexibility enables the system to work in actual practice.

Somewhat akin to this concept of flexibility is the system of priorities implicit in the planning. For instance, the Gosplan might plan for a certain output of building materials and a labor force of so many people to carry out the construction program. If the plans for labor force, productivity, and materials supply work out, the successful completion of all the projects listed, from giant dams to factories to schools and housing, should be realized. But if it appears in the process of plan fulfillment that not all this program can actually be accomplished, the low-priority construction projects (housing has been a traditional example) are dropped and the approximation, or error, involved in the original plan is corrected *ex post* by sacrificing the low-priority objectives.

5. *The task of planning coordination in the Soviet economy is less complicated than it would be in the United States economy because of the relatively low level of consumption and the nature of the goals the planners have set for the economy.* Consumption levels have been so low in the Soviet economy that it has not been difficult to determine what consumer goods ought to be produced. A simple list of the basic necessities with no frills has been the obvious answer and, even if the various elements in this market basket were not in optimal proportions or were of poor quality, they were taken off the market easily enough and satisfied real needs of the population. This is coming to be less and less true, of course, and has led to problems to which we will return later. The other components of demand, the investment goods and the military items which are so important in the pattern of Soviet production, are much more stable in composition than the consumer demands of an economy — and are therefore more susceptible to forecasting. Hence the required amounts of such goods can be programmed relatively easily. Incidentally, these features of the Soviet economy are shared by any underdeveloped country embarking on a program of industrialization. As a result, the difficulties of coordination which might make economic planning inappropriate for an economy with high levels of consumption (such as ours) are less important for the Russians or, by extension, for those underdeveloped countries that might be tempted to choose the Soviet planning approach to industrialization.

6. *Finally, it should be emphasized that the planning process does not work perfectly.* Often various limits and directives assigned to an enterprise contain inconsistencies; parts of a plan may be changed without correcting the other parts that will be affected; and plans will fail to specify what is to be done with output or where a plant is to get the materials it needs. A balance is more nearly achieved on paper than in reality. Despite such mistakes, however, the planning process does what should probably be considered an acceptable job of coordinating supplies and demands.

Soviet Experiments with Input-Output. These Soviet mechanisms for getting the plan balanced seem to have worked so far, though the job done is far from perfect and it absorbs a large amount of resources. But the continued feasibility of these mechanisms is strongly threatened today by the fact of growth. As the economy gets bigger, the balancing job takes more effort, becomes more frantic, and results in more costly mistakes. Several Russians have made eloquent predictions that unless something is done, the annual balancing process will become less and less workable and the burden of staffing the planning offices will become intolerable. Faced with this prospect, the Russians have recently become interested in input-output as a technique that might enable them to deal with this problem of coordination more effectively. For many years developments in economic thought in the capitalist countries were ignored in the U.S.S.R., except for an occasional ritual pronouncement to the effect that some bit of bourgeois theorizing was a hopeless attempt to shore up capitalism against its impending collapse. After Stalin's death, however, Soviet economists, like other technicians, were encouraged to study developments in the capitalist world in search of ideas that might be of use to them. One of the discoveries was input-output, and indeed a whole family of "mathematical techniques," and the Russians are now experimenting with applying them to their problem of balancing supplies and demands. It will be useful at this point to describe what they have done along these lines and to speculate on whether input-output can save them. But this requires a somewhat fuller look at input-output to see what it does and does not do.

Once the interrelationships between different sectors have been laid bare in an input-output table such as that in Table 3.1, it is possible to extract from the system a mathematical model of production interrelationships. Remember that the uses shown represent two different categories — final demand and intermediate demand. Each intermediate demand can be interpreted as the product of two factors — for example, the number of tons of steel required for the machinery industry is the product of multiplying the millions of dollars' worth of machinery to be produced times the number of tons of steel required per million dollars' worth of machinery output. Final demands are autonomous — i.e., they are determined by considerations outside these input-output relationships. The main condition to be satisfied in the system is that the output of any industry be large enough to cover all the demands on it. To take steel as an example, a statement of the following form can be made for each industry. "The total output of steel needs to be just large enough so that it can cover whatever steel is needed for all intermediate users (each of these needs being expressed as the output of the using industry times the amount of steel needed per unit of its output), with enough left over to cover the demands of households, government and other final users."

Translated into symbols, this statement takes the following form: $X_1 = a_{11}X_1 + a_{12}X_2 + a_{13}X_3 + a_{14}X_4 \ldots a_{1,13}X_{13}$ + Final demands, where X stands for the total output of some industry (*which* industry being indicated by the subscript) and the a's are input coefficients. For example, a_{13} means the amount of the product of industry 1 required per unit of output of industry 3. If industry 1 is the steel industry and industry 3 the automobile industry, then a_{13} stands for the tons of steel needed to produce one automobile. In this equation, each X represents an unknown, i.e., the level of output for that industry. In the input-output matrix of Table 3.1 there would be thirteen such unknowns. Since a similar equation can be set up for each industry, there are as many equations as there are industry output levels to be determined. Once we have specified what is desired in the way of final demands, the set of equations can then be solved to find the output level required for each industry. This required set of output levels may or may not be feasible depending on the capacity limits of each industry and on some overall constraints such as labor. The procedure then is to experiment with alternative combinations of final demands to find the best one that is also feasible. With modern computers it becomes possible to carry out this exploration of feasible alternatives very rapidly, even for very large systems.

Input-output thus seems a close enough analogue to what the Russians are already doing to make it a feasible replacement for their present trial and error balancing. At the same time it would be much faster and more flexible. Soviet economists have been experimenting with the construction of input-output matrices for the Soviet economy for some years now. The construction of an input-output table is a complicated endeavor, involving a tremendous job of data collection and of finding satisfactory definitional compromises to fit the complexities of a real economy into this rather abstract scheme. The Russians have prepared a succession of input-output tables of increasing size and refinement. The latest stage in their experimentation is to use the input-output table to generate the levels of output and its allocation implicit in the plan targets for some future year and then to check these against the plan worked out in the actual planning process. The results are said to be encouragingly close but the Russians are apparently not yet willing to trust actual operational planning to the computer.

More important, their interest in using input-output to plan the economy has now been altered somewhat by new developments. To understand these, a brief detour is required here to explain the limitations of input-output and its relationships to other mathematical techniques which the planners are now considering.

Implicit in the input-output description of economic relationships are some peculiar assumptions about production — the important one here being that the production of a ton of steel takes a fixed menu of inputs and that no substitution of one input for another is possible. That may be all right as an approximation but is not really true. To produce a KWH of electric power, for instance, substitution of one fuel for another is possible — one can reduce the expenditure of coal per KWH by using more natural gas. Thus input-output is an unrealistically restrictive framework. Suppose that balancing via input-output shows that electric power is a bottleneck because there is a shortage of coal. The input-output approach will not suggest that the bottleneck could be broken by substituting gas for coal. Input-output is thus solely a balancing technique and completely ignores some of the important aspects of optimizing the allocation of resources and choosing the most efficient methods of production.

Another mathematical technique, known as linear programming, resembles input-output in many ways but is different in precisely this respect. It acknowledges that there is more than one technique for producing electric power (or any other output) and that these techniques differ from each other by different input coefficients. Electric power can be produced in hydroelectric stations with one set of coefficients, in gas fired thermal stations with another, or in coal fired stations with still another. The linear programming approach broadens the balancing process to consider not only what levels of output of each commodity are required but also, for each one, what combination of alternative technologies should be used to economize on the scarcest factors. The Russians were slower to appreciate the relevance of linear programming than to appreciate the relevance of input-output, even though, paradoxically, the theory of linear programming was first developed in the U.S.S.R. Because their present balancing procedure is so little concerned with the optimizing problem that linear programming is concerned with, they did not at first even appreciate the issue. There is also a doctrinal problem in that there are ideas about value and price implicit in linear programming that seem inconsistent with Marxist doctrine. (More will be said about this below.) But these difficulties have now been largely overcome and the Russians are thinking about not simply mechanizing the balancing process by using computers and input-output but about incorporating optimizing features via linear programming. The Russians are now planning to set up a network of very large computing centers controlled from one master center in Moscow in order to improve their ability to handle and process economic information and utilize it in some such way. The aggregate computing capacity of the system would be something like the joint capacity of all the computers in existence in the United States in the mid-sixties. With this much capacity, the Russians could formulate and handle the annual balancing problem in an optimizing way. The details are too technical to go into here, but the system would both balance supply and demand for all kinds of outputs and optimize current allocation by recognizing that substitution is possible and ensuring that resources were allocated to the uses where their productivity would be highest.

Most observers outside the U.S.S.R. express some doubts that this scheme will ever work in the way they now visualize it but there is no doubt that the Russians take it seriously and are engaged in the research work it will require, both in terms of developing the computational capacity and in continuing the experimentation with input-output tables and linear programming that will precede any attempt to make it operational. They are now fully convinced that their present system of handling the balancing problem in the annual plan is becoming insupportable but they hope that the computer and these mathematical techniques will provide a means of automating it in a way that will keep the basic principles of central balancing and the command economy intact.

4

Strategic and Operational Decision Making

The process of annual plan making is bracketed, as we have already explained, in its time dimensions and in the level of the decision-making units involved, by two other spheres of decision making which contribute importantly to the allocation of resources. On one side is a group of design decisions which fix many variables in the economic system for extended periods of time and to which decisions made in the annual balancing process must conform. On the other side is a sphere of decision making which involves essentially short-term variations and adjustments at lower levels of administration. Decision makers in this sphere settle in detail and often alter the decisions made in the other two spheres. This latter area corresponds to what the Russians call control of plan fulfillment, but "control" suggests a process more precise and rigorous than the actual one. In fact, the methods used to "control" plan fulfillment really just set the stage for a new sphere of decision making on the part of those to whom the plan commands are addressed. This chapter considers, with respect to both of these areas, how decisions are made and whether they are made rationally.

Design Decision Making

There is a well demarcated sphere of planning in the Sovie Union which the Russians call project making (*proektirovanie*)

Project making is more or less equivalent to the design of productive facilities and equipment, as in the following illustrations. In the process of working out the plan for the power industry, there comes a point at which someone must design the new generating facilities that will make possible an expansion of electric power output. Once an effort to expand agricultural output by a big increase in fertilizer supply has been decided upon, chemical engineers will have to choose and design a complex of raw material sources, producing and transforming technologies, and equipment and procedures for using the fertilizer. Technological progress is sustained by continuing efforts to design new machines (new truck models, for example) or complexes of machines such as a computer-controlled production line in a machinery plant. Once an oil reservoir is discovered, it is necessary to work out a "project" for producing the oil from it, a project which will cover such variables as well spacing, the kind of equipment to be used, and whether special techniques, such as artificial pressure maintenance, are to be used. The project-making institutions which make these decisions in the Soviet Union take many forms — some are research organizations in the Academy of Sciences, some are attached to the central organs of administration, some are located closer to the bottom of the administrative pyramid. Large projects usually involve the cooperation of a number of such organizations.

In defining the task of the project maker, the planners specify a few main variables. They may fix the location or specify the level of output the new facility is to have. But even within the limitations imposed by such directives, the project-making planners have a great deal of latitude in choosing among technological alternatives. Those designing the chemical process may have the choice of alternative raw materials and production processes. Each of these alternatives has rather different impacts upon the economy. The engineer usually has a choice between capital-intensive solutions, which save labor but impose bigger claims on available capital supplies, and other variants which save on capital but require more labor or other current inputs. In designing new electric power plants, the temperature and pressure at which steam is circulated in the system are important technical parameters which the engineer can manipulate. The choices he makes will have important implications for the specifications required of the materials

used in constructing the equipment and for the thermal efficiency of the station. The point is that technology offers such a range of choice that a mere specification of the general characteristics of a project leaves many questions unanswered. The designers who finally turn out blueprints and specifications must themselves make many decisions and these decisions affect importantly the allocation of resources. Whether these decisions about resource allocation are made correctly turns mainly on two sub-problems: (1) whether the Russians understand the economic issues involved in a given problem and (2) whether the institutional setting and the available information will permit the planners to make the correct decisions. It is to Marxism, of course, that the Russians have usually turned for guidance on understanding economic issues but they have in Marxism an economic theory which is in many respects erroneous and in other respects seriously incomplete. Their commitment to this body of doctrine may interfere with their understanding of important issues involved in economizing and choosing among alternatives. And even when their theoretical analysis of an economic problem is correct, the planners may still be unable to make correct decisions because they lack the kind of information needed for a rational decision or because they are subjected to pressures and constraints which force them to act irrationally. Anything approaching a comprehensive survey of the rationality of choice in this sphere of Soviet decision making would be too great a task to undertake here. But it is possible to describe some typical cases to illustrate the obstacles which the Soviet economic system has put in the way of sensible project-making decisions.

Capital Allocation. Project makers almost always face a choice about the "capital intensity" of a project. (Capital intensity refers to the value of capital tied up in some production facility in relation to the value of its annual output. The more dollars' worth of resources tied up in capital per dollars' worth of output per year, the higher the capital intensity.) The planners responsible for designing factories or machinery, for choosing between traditional or automated production lines, or for designing railroads, for example, constantly find that if they could have permission to commit more capital to these projects, the cost per unit of output in terms of current operating costs would decrease. Consider, for instance, the problem of a project maker in the electric power industry who must decide whether an assigned increment of generating capacity should be met by building a steam station or a hydroelectric station. When he estimates the costs for the two alternatives, he may find something like this:

	Steam Station	Hydroelectric Station
Capacity	50 thousand KW	50 thousand KW
Initial Investment	50 million rubles	100 million rubles
Annual Operating Costs	25 " "	20 " "
Fuel	10 " "	0 " "
Labor	10 " "	5 " "
Depreciation	5 " "	10 " "
Other	0 " "	5 " "

The hydroelectric station will require an initial investment of 100 million rubles, compared to only 50 million rubles for a steam station of the same capacity. But once this investment is made, the operating costs per kilowatt hour of electricity produced will be appreciably lower forever after. Note that since depreciation has been figured in as one of the costs, one can assume that this station or a successor, financed from the depreciation allowances, can remain in operation indefinitely without additional investment. The hydro station will have no cost for fuel and there will be savings in other items, such as labor, as well. This possibility of cutting future operating costs by increasing capital investment in a project today occurs in many other situations. It should be noted that in the usual situation there are not just two alternatives, as our example suggests, but a whole succession of variants for any project, offering a more or less continuous trade-off between investment requirements and operating costs. Where along this continuum is the optimal capital intensity?

This problem as formulated by a firm in the capitalist economy would be different from our example in an important respect. In the capitalist economy there would be an interest charge for capital, and interest payments would be one element of the annual operating costs. Increases in the capital intensity of a project add to the annual operating costs in the form of interest charges, and increases in capital intensity are carried to the point where the savings in operating costs are just offset by the additional interest payments to which the extra investment commits the firm. In the calculation shown above, the project maker has not included interest as an operating cost since there is no interest charge for the use of capital in the Soviet economy. Investments are generally financed by means of interest-free grants from state sources. The absence of an interest charge in the Soviet economy is based on Marxian economic theory. According to Marx's theory of value, only labor creates value and such returns as those which the capitalist gets on his investment or the landlord for the use of his land represent exploitation rather than compensation for some productive service which has been supplied by the capital or the land. Capital contributes nothing to production and to a believer in Marxian theory it would therefore seem absurd to require payment for the use of capital once the power of the capitalists is overthrown.

This Marxian interpretation of capital and interest is erroneous; capital is productive in the sense that the addition of capital to a given process increases the output. Moreover, capital is scarce and some rule is required for allocating it to the most productive uses. In the capitalist economy the interest charge serves both as a payment for the productive services of capital and as a means for rationing it. Unless the prospective user of capital finds that it will increase his output or will cut his costs enough to be worth the interest he must pay for it, he will forego using it and indeed cannot obtain it. Thus the rate of interest is a means by which capital is rationed out to those uses and in those amounts that will maximize its overall productivity.

In the Soviet economy the basic circumstance that capital is both productive and scarce still holds. It is true that in the Soviet system there is no need for the state to pay interest to attract capital. Interest is not necessary to persuade people to save since the state can compel savings by various fiscal and pricing devices. But the problem remains of assuring that capital be used in the best way, that the project maker in the example above not choose the hydroelectric station if the extra 50 million rubles which it requires could be more productively employed elsewhere. Thus we return to the question of what rule decision makers should follow in deciding how far to move toward the more capital intensive variants of any project. Clearly, it will not do just to tell them to choose the variant that would minimize operating costs. The response would be that the sum of investment resources requested for all the projects being considered would far outstrip the amount available. If the irrationality and the extra work of an arbitrary allocation by some higher level decision makers is to be avoided, it is necessary to provide some rule that each decision maker can apply on his own and in Soviet planning practice there gradually has emerged what is called the "pay-off period" approach. In considering possible variants of a given investment project, the project maker asks how long it will take for the savings in operating costs in the more capital intensive variant to cover the additional capital investment which it requires. In the example mentioned above, for instance, the hydroelectric power station requires 50 million rubles more investment than a steam station of the same capacity but its annual operating costs are 5 million rubles less. The pay-off period for the additional capital investment would thus be ten years. To guide project makers in these choices it has been customary to establish the rule that additional investment in such cases can be justified only if the pay-off period for the additional capital investment does not exceed some stipulated number of years. The number of years stipulated is not uniform but varies from industry to industry.

A moment's reflection will show that the pay-off period is essentially the rate of interest turned upside down. A recoupment period of five years, for instance, means that the return to the additional capital invested (the return being measured as the value of resources saved) amounts each year to 20 per cent of the investment. Or in other words, the productivity of the capital in this case is 20 per cent. If the authorities set a rule for plant designers that the payoff period must be no more than five years, they are in effect saying that capital should not be used unless the return to it is at least 20 per cent. Thus the condemned rate of interest is brought in through the back door. In the early postwar years, the anti-Marxist implication of this practice was realized and it was officially condemned by the Marxist theoreticians. There followed a long controversy in which the necessity for some such device for capital allocation was made clear and in the end it was decided to allow the pay-off period approach to be used openly and universally. In going through this evolution the Russians have not declared that Marx was wrong in his labor theory of value, but they have come to realize that the theory must be ignored when it conflicts with the demands of rationality in this practical problem.

It should not by any means be concluded that official acceptance of the pay-off period approach means that the Russians actually achieve a rational allocation of capital. Having surmounted the difficulties in theoretical analysis, they have still not established the institutions for implementing the new understanding. No reasonable pay-off period has yet been figured out and in practice the Russians charge different rates of interest to different users of capital. This is wrong because it means that some planner might conclude that he should use an extra thousand rubles of capital to save 50 rubles per year (i.e., if the pay-out period allowed in his industry were 12.5 years or more), whereas someone else who might have a more productive use for that thousand rubles of investment funds would decide against it because he measured the use against a shorter pay-out period norm. Nevertheless, the Soviet economists are groping their way toward a more rational system of decision making in this area. Once the issue is understood analytically, then the way is open to reform the rules, to induce the decision makers to make decisions that will be rational from an economy-wide point of view.

The most recent step in the evolution of the Soviet attitude on this problem is official acceptance of the idea that an interest charge should be levied against enterprises for the capital they use, with a corresponding inclusion of interest in prices. The more liberal economists had come to understand the rationale of an interest charge and had slowly won agreement with their view that it was an indispensable guide in economic decision making. In the planning reforms approved in 1965, such a charge was officially accepted, though there is still much confusion and controversy as to how it should be introduced in practice.

The Turbodrill. In addition to the problem of designing whole plants, there is a problem of designing equipment and the choices made have an important impact on efficiency. For the most part

Soviet project makers have simply copied western equipment designs. Indeed they have often followed western patterns in designing whole factories, though often with some adaptation to their own situations. But there are cases in which they have developed technological processes on their own — one of the most interesting examples being the turbodrill used for drilling oil and gas wells. In most of the world, oil wells are drilled by the rotary method in which a rock-cutting bit attached to the bottom of a long string of steel pipe is rotated in the hole by rotating the pipe. Drilling mud is forced down the pipe string, flows through and around the bit and back to the surface through the space between the pipe wall and the side of the hole. This circulating mud cools the bit, flushes the crushed rock fragments out of the hole, and counteracts the pressures encountered in the well. Rotary drilling technology is very demanding in terms of its requirements for quality in the steel pipe and for precision in the machining of the tool joints by which the lengths of pipe are screwed together. The drilling performance achieved in the Soviet oil industry has in the past been quite unsatisfactory, partly because the Russians were never able to cope very effectively with these quality problems. The low quality of their pipe and bits meant a large amount of time lost in breakdowns due to broken pipe, lost tools, etc. The Russians sought to bypass these difficulties by a radical change in the technology, i.e., by developing the turbodrill. In the turbodrill the bit is powered by a long slim turbine placed at the bottom of the string of drill pipe. The mud which is pumped down the drill string serves as the working fluid to operate the turbine. Thus the turbodrill can be thought of as a kind of hydraulic system for transmitting power to the bottom of the hole in place of the mechanical transmission principle used in traditional rotary drilling. The turbodrill has in fact enabled the Russians to make considerable progress in improving productivity in drilling, though that story will not be pursued here. We are interested in the turbodrill as an illustration of the problem Soviet project makers have in making design decisions and of the errors they make.

In the design of a hydraulic system like that of the turbodrill there are many choices to be made concerning pressures, rate of flow of the working fluid, the shape of the turbine vanes, and the diameter of the drill pipe. In choosing values for these parameters the engineers who designed the turbodrill settled them on the basis of the only criterion they knew — i.e., mechanical efficiency. They chose values for the design parameters with an eye to minimizing the amount of power lost through friction and to maximizing the power delivered to the bit at the bottom of the hole, thereby speeding up the rate at which the bit cut through the rock. Most of the costs of drilling a well are proportional to time so that by drilling the hole in a shorter period of time, its cost can be reduced. But despite this general economic rationale justifying their goal of engineering efficiency, the designers of the turbodrill technology overlooked some important considerations relevant to economic efficiency. Mechanical efficiency required that the turbine and bit rotate at a high speed and this shortened the life of bits. The number of feet drilled by a bit before it wore out and had to be replaced was drastically reduced. Shorter bit life means a larger number of bits required to drill a hole to a given depth and an increase in the number of times the drill string must be pulled out of the hole to replace the bit. Such a round trip is a time-consuming operation since it involves raising the string the length of one joint, which is unscrewed and stacked in the derrick, and repeating the process until the whole string is out. A new bit is then lowered to the bottom by repeating the whole process in reverse. While time is taken out for this "round trip" to replace the bit, the hole is not getting any deeper, of course. Thus while the design engineers were pursuing their goal of maximizing the mechanical efficiency of the process and maximizing the rate at which the bit penetrated the rock while actually drilling, the economic goal was being interfered with since the loss in time from extra round trips more than offset the time gained from pushing the bit through the rock more rapidly. The Russians have now recognized that they made a serious mistake here and are seeking to correct it, though this will take considerable time since their preoccupation with the turbodrill kept them from doing research and development work on rotary methods. This situation, where design decisions are in the hands of engineers who do not fully understand or appreciate the *economic* issues involved, is common in the Soviet Union and the sacrifice of economic efficiency to some engineering prejudice is a characteristic weakness in this sphere of decision making.

Scale, Specialization, and Location of Plants.   Project makers must deal with an extremely complicated group of questions in deciding where to locate industrial plants and how large and how specialized to make them. The optimum size of plant in a given industry is determined by such considerations as the savings that come from large-scale production, transportation costs of shipping the product to the customers in a market area of a given size, flexibility in service to customers. In most kinds of industrial processes, enlarging the plant, up to a certain point, brings reductions in costs because of the possibilities of better organization and other "economies of scale." There is, however, a point beyond which further expansion brings no economies in production costs but requires that the plant must serve a larger and larger market area. The resulting increase in transport charges will affect delivery cost adversely. An indication of the best size for a plant for any given industry is obtained by balancing off all of these different factors against one another. The capitalist attempts to evaluate all such factors in deciding the size and location of his plant and, in the long run, the force of competition works to eliminate those producers whose calculations did not meet the demands of rationality.

It is often argued that the Soviet system, on the other hand, is prone to expensive errors in this area of decision making. For example, policies of plant size and location in one important branch of the economy — the iron and steel industry — have been carefully analyzed in one study with the following conclusions. In the thirties, the designers of iron and steel units strove to make them as large and as specialized as possible in order to cut production costs to the minimum. In doing this, however, they more or less ignored a number of important factors which should have been taken into account in deciding the best size of plant from the overall national economic point of view. Rolling mills, for instance, were designed to be so big and so specialized that a single rolling mill could produce the entire output of a particular item for the whole country. This meant very low production costs for that output, of course, but by the time the item was delivered to customers all over the Soviet Union the delivered cost was extremely high. The geographical location and the specialization of the rolling mill seriously restricted the responsiveness of the iron and steel industry to the needs of its customers. Because many customers were located at points far distant, it was difficult for them to communicate with or to influence the rolling mill which was producing the goods they needed. That this could happen was partly the result of the institutional structure of the Soviet economy. The motivations of planners in Soviet industry are mostly concerned with costs and volume of output and planners follow policies in designing plants which will improve these indicators as much as possible. It made no difference to the designers of iron and steel mills that their decisions would involve extra work for the railroad system or that customers would be inconvenienced. That was the worry of the customers and of the railroads. Toward the end of the thirties the folly of this approach to planning became obvious. It was found that in a number of areas of the economy the emphasis on large-scale plants and neglect of transportation costs and customer service were wholly undesirable. There was official condemnation and a campaign against "gigantomania," i.e., a bias in favor of giant plants, and planners were instructed in the future to design smaller plants scattered throughout the Soviet Union.

Indeed it may well be that in this case, as often happens in the Soviet economy, the policy makers at the top went too far in the other direction in their zeal to correct past errors. One of the most obvious results of the gigantomania was an excessive load on the transportation system. In order to correct this, the Russian leaders announced a new policy in industrial location which was to emphasize regional self-sufficiency. Fairly large regions of the country were to be more or less self-sufficient with regard to production of many important items. In order to enforce this policy there was a reform in railroad freight rates which penalized shipments beyond a certain planned average distance for a particular commodity. Thus, for instance, it was planned that the average length of haul for coal should be about 700 kilometers, and when coal was shipped farther, the rates began to rise very sharply. This was intended to discourage the shipment of coal from one region to another and thus to stimulate its production within each of the self-sufficient regions. But, in their efforts to make each of these regions self-sufficient, the Russians failed to take full advantage of the possibilities of interregional specialization of labor.

The reason for this kind of panacea approach is that the decision makers in this sphere often lack the detailed information required to permit them to take all the relevant factors into account. Their response is usually to operate according to some more or less crude rules of thumb. Such rules are likely to cover only some of the variables in any situation — as when the steel industry planners set up cost and output as goals and neglected transport costs and the needs of customers.

Execution of Plans

The allocation of resources decided upon in the annual plan and implicit in the kind of decisions which strategic decision makers have made about projects is not necessarily realized in practice. Still another class of decision makers — management at the level of the enterprise charged with carrying out the commands of the central planners — has an important influence on the outcome. As the Russians are fond of repeating, planning is only the first stage of economic administration. No matter how carefully the plan has been drawn up, it means nothing until it is executed. And it is worth emphasizing that it is people who carry the plan to completion. In the Soviet system the people who have the responsibility of carrying out the plan are bureaucrats, employees of the state, and the private profit motive which plays so important a role in the free enterprise economy is absent. How can these people be effectively persuaded to fulfill the plans drawn up by the regime and to exercise their decision-making power in a manner consonant with achieving the goals of the leaders?

Administrative Structure of the Soviet Economy.   An explanation of the forces that make Soviet managers work hard at their task can be begun best by a brief description of the administrative structure of the Soviet economy. The Soviet economy is organized on the hierarchical principle. There is a pyramid of authority in which orders come down from the top and responsibility flows up. At the very top of the structure is the Council of Ministers of the U.S.S.R. This is the level at which the general objectives of the economy are established and general plans laid out. At the next level down, the Soviet economy during most of its history has been partitioned up for administrative purposes into a number of sectors, such as agriculture, transportation, industry — electric power, coal, etc. — and authority and control over each sector has been lodged in what was once called a People's Commissariat and then later a ministry of that sector of the economy. These ministries and the ministers which head them have been directly under the control of the Council of Ministers. Most of these ministries have been controlled from a main office located in Moscow. The ministries were so large, however, that the minister in Moscow could not possibly personally supervise and run such a huge collection of economic activities. The Ministry of Ferrous Metals, for instance, constituted a monstrous industrial empire, with jurisdiction over thousands of enterprises including blast furnaces, ore mines, coal mines, coke plants, lumbering operations, a very large marketing organization, research institutions, and an educational network. Moreover, these enterprises are scattered from one end of the Soviet Union to the other. In order to manage such complex industrial units, the Russians created an intermediate level of authority under the ministry called the chief administration (the Russian term is *glavnoe upravlenie,* usually shortened to *glavk.*). These chief administrations were assigned responsibility for particular aspects of each ministry's operating activities — some of them in charge of specialized branches of production, others concerned with staff functions such as procurement, marketing, or research. There might be still another level of authority and control beneath the chief administration, consisting of "combines" or "trusts" which ordinarily contain a number of industrial plants or mines. Then at the very bottom of the administrative hierarchy, there is the individual firm or enterprise. The man in charge of the industrial firm is called the director and it is his actions and motivations and those of his immediate subordinates which most directly influence the quality, the level, and the rate of growth of Soviet production.

The reader will readily perceive that there are similarities between this structure and that of large firms in the American economy. A big American corporation operates a number of individual establishments, often widely dispersed geographically. It is generally found convenient to group these individual establishments into larger aggregates, usually called divisions, specialized by the nature of the product, problems of marketing, or some other common feature of their activity. Within this structure, certain functions, such as finance, advertising, labor relations, sometimes even purchasing or production planning, may be removed from the control of management of an individual establishment and handled by special units at higher levels in the corporate structure. The analogy is far from complete, of course, since only the largest American corporations have operations approaching in scope the area of an economy encompassed by even a single Soviet ministry. Therefore the administrative problems of even the biggest U.S. corporation are multiplied many-fold in the Soviet system. Nevertheless, it is helpful to think of the Soviet planned economy as equivalent to one giant corporation which embraces all the units of a national economy under a single administration.

The system of ministries just described characterized the Soviet structure until 1957. In that year this pyramid of authority was changed somewhat, although the hierarchical principle remains as before. What happened was that in industry and construction ministries were abolished and were replaced by regional economic councils. In other words, the division of industry into special branches according to the product produced or the technology employed was replaced by a partitioning on a geographical basis. (A few of the industrial ministries were retained and ministries also remain in many nonindustrial sectors of the economy such as transportation. Certain functions which could be performed best for an industry as a whole on a nation-wide scale, such as technical progress, were left in the hands of still other central bodies, the state committees.) Each of these geographical units was run by an "economic council" having under its jurisdiction plants from a number of branches of industry. Ordinarily these enterprises were grouped into a number of chief administrations under the economic council, specialized by branch of industry. This change from a branch basis to a territorial basis in industrial organization had some important implications for the effectiveness of planning and control but obviously it in no way destroyed the hierarchical structure described earlier. Since the end of 1965, there has been a return to the branch principle, under ministries, and an abolition of the regional economic councils.

Nature of the Soviet Enterprise. Next we want to consider what sort of entity the bottom rung of this administrative ladder — the Soviet enterprise — is. In certain respects it is not much different from a capitalist corporation. It gets its resources in the first instance as a grant from the state but subsequently it is to proceed more or less on its own, covering its expenses out of the revenues from sale of its output. The things it produces it sells for money and the things it consumes it pays for in money. It is expected to carry on accounting and to determine its own profit or loss. The director of this enterprise, like the officers of a corporation, is in effect a steward of someone else's property and is held responsible for the operation and conservation of that property. The main difference is that in the Soviet case the steward is responsible to the Soviet state rather than to a group of private citizens. This stewardship, the responsibility for managing the enterprise to produce as much as possible as efficiently as possible, the Russians call economic accountability, or *khozraschet*.

Now that we have described this environment, the question of control over plan fulfillment can be restated somewhat more specifically with reference to the group of people who hold various positions in this line of command. We are most interested in the role of enterprise management but clearly it is also important to ask something about the motivations of people above the manager and about his means for controlling the people subordinate to him. How can the managers in this system be made to shun waste, care about efficiency, take upon themselves the trouble of introducing more efficient methods in their plants?

There is certainly good reason to suspect that these desirable results will not come just as a matter of course. The goals of the managers do not necessarily coincide with those of the regime. Why should these bureaucrats break their backs so that Stalin can build monuments to himself in Moscow, so that Khrushchev can extend economic aid to Egypt, or so that Russians a generation later can have a thirty-five-hour work week? Obviously it is necessary to structure the setting in which the manager works so that he will do his best to fulfill the commands and decisions emanating from higher levels. He will also have to be given a set of decision rules so that with regard to issues and problems not specifically noted in the plans he will make decisions that are rational in the light of the overall functioning of the economy. The solution which the regime has used can be described crudely by the familiar idea of the carrot and the stick, although this simple conception scarcely does justice to the intricacies of the system of both positive and negative incentives which the manager faces.

Material Rewards of Managers.   Successful managers in the Soviet economy, those who fulfill and overfulfill the plans assigned to them, are well rewarded in material terms. In addition to being well paid, managers may enjoy other perquisites such as a home, the use of an automobile, travel on expense accounts, vacations at resorts, and so on. Many of these are rewards that money alone cannot buy in the Soviet Union — they come only with certain official positions. The differentiation of rewards to make them proportional to performance is achieved largely by a system of bonuses or premia which the manager and his staff receive in addition to their base salaries. There are two main kinds of bonuses. One is for fulfilling the plan generally and, in addition, there are many specific bonus schemes in individual branches of industry based on specific problems of those branches. For instance, in the electric power industry there have been specific bonuses for reducing the input of fuel per kilowatt-hour of power generated and in many branches there are special bonuses for improving the quality of goods. Another important class is bonus systems for the introduction of new technology and for inventions.

The system of premia given to enterprise management for plan fulfillment is rather elaborate, involving both cost and output indicators, and with varying rates depending on how the plan is formulated in a particular industry. Hence it is difficult to make generalizations about how premia are calculated. But a typical scheme might involve bonus payments for fulfilling the output plan equal to 15 per cent of the base salary, with an additional 1.5 per cent of base salary for each tenth of a percentage point by which costs are reduced compared with the plan. In some branches there are also bonuses for overfulfilling the output plan and these are paid at a rate of 3 to 5 per cent of base salary per percent of overfulfillment. This system of bonuses applies not only to the director but to his main assistants as well. (In 1964 and 1965, in connection with the experimental use of profit as a success indicator in some enterprises of light industry, premia for these enterprises were made a function of how much profit they earned. But this is essentially an exception to the more general pattern described.) The trend in recent years has been to reduce somewhat the emphasis placed on bonuses and to reduce the share of bonuses in total managerial compensation but it remains an important element in the incomes of all the top officials of the enterprise. The share of premia in total payments to managerial personnel in industry in recent years has been from 10 to 15 per cent. This is the average, of course, and many people earn far larger bonuses. Many people do not get bonuses since not all people successfully fill the plan — thus obviously for some the bonuses are relatively much more important.

We have emphasized the material rewards which motivate the managerial elite because these are probably the ones that work most powerfully in assuring dedicated managerial effort. But the motivation of managers in the Soviet economy is undoubtedly complex, just as in a capitalist corporation. Mixed in with the concern for material success is a host of other motivations and incentives — the desire to serve society, to hold power, to exercise one's initiative and energy in some creative way. To convince oneself that such a system of incentives will draw forth adequate managerial effort, one should think of its similarities to the goals that motivate the "organization men" in American corporations.

The Soviet official has traditionally also had to keep in mind some extremely harsh negative sanctions for poor performance. For American management, punishment for failure scarcely exists. As corporations have become larger and more bureaucratized, their managerial staffs have been insulated from even the traditional negative sanction of the free enterprise economy, namely, loss of one's job. Whatever subtle punishments the status system may impose on a member of the management team who fails in the performance of his responsibilities, he is not much more in danger of being fired or demoted than a government employee. In the Soviet Union, on the other hand, insecurity is one of the major elements of the managerial environment. Loss of one's job is the least of the evils that can befall responsible people in the Soviet managerial structure. They are held to a very strict accountability for their actions and are often judged arbitrarily. Failure to achieve fulfillment of the planned targets may bring an accusation of criminal negligence or of economic crimes against the state and the responsible persons could be imprisoned or shot. At the same time, a manager's best efforts to meet the plan targets may lead him afoul of the multitudinous legal prohibitions that circumscribe his freedom of action. For instance, the materials supply system works ineffectively and he may have to resort to illegal means of procuring materials in order to fulfill the plan. Many of these legal restraints are not rigorously enforced but enterprise officials always place themselves in a potentially dangerous position by violating them. Negative sanctions work best if they lurk more or less in the background; making managers excessively insecure defeats the objective of keeping them as productive as possible. In general, the trend since Stalin's death has been to mitigate the elements of arbitrariness and terror in the system of negative sanctions.

Problems in the Administration of Incentives

This system of incentives means that Soviet managers are highly motivated to try to fulfill the plans which are handed down to them. They have every reason to do their best to meet the goals of the plan and to convince their superiors that they are doing a good job. In such a system, however, two important problems arise.

1. The first is cheating. When the pressures to fulfill the plan are so strong, there is a strong temptation for managers to fulfill the plan by what has been called "simulation." The idea is to achieve the appearance of plan fulfillment if not the substance. A plan can be fulfilled in more than one way. One of the easiest methods is to arrange things beforehand so that one has an easy plan to fulfill. In the process of planning, enterprises propose targets for output, costs, labor force, and capital investment. It is not surprising, therefore, that enterprises look upon this part of the process as an important bargaining situation. They bargain for a small output goal, a generous allocation of materials, as large a labor force as possible. The reason it is possible to carry on such

bargaining is that it is very difficult for people at higher levels to know what the performance of an enterprise really should be. Another more blatant form of cheating is to falsify reports of plan fulfillment. A Soviet enterprise reports monthly, quarterly, and annually on its progress in fulfilling its plan. What is to prevent the manager from drawing up a very optimistic report claiming that he has overfulfilled the plan? And if he does, how will his superiors ever find out that the report on plan fulfillment is falsified?

2. The second big problem is setting up some system of measuring how successfully a plan is fulfilled. The plan specifies a great many targets the manager is to achieve and in the nature of things the plan is never fulfilled exactly. Therefore those who evaluate plan fulfillment must establish some set of priorities for relating underfulfillment of one goal to overfulfillment of another. As we shall see, it is difficult to establish a set of priorities that will always lead the enterprise managers to do the things that are best from the national economic point of view.

Falsification. Given the pressure to obtain an easy plan and the temptation to falsify reported achievements, how can the regime forestall such actions? Essentially the regime has adopted the hard-boiled attitude that it is impossible to take at face value the word of people at lower levels and it has constructed many separate channels for checking on the performance of managers and for placing pressure on managers to tighten up plans. One of the distinctive things about the Soviet economy is the great number of agencies that in some way check on or examine in detail the work and reports of enterprises. The most important of these control agencies is the agency which stands immediately above the enterprise in the administrative hierarchy. (An example would be the chief administration or *glavk* described above.) The chief administration demands a large volume of statistical and accounting reports from enterprises under its jurisdiction. The very completeness and volume of this reported information in itself makes falsification somewhat difficult. All the different aspects of the performance of a plant are mutually interrelated and falsifying reports on one aspect requires that other parts be falsified as well. There is a variety of internal checks among the different indicators of performance that an enterprise reports, and attempted falsification runs the risk of detection because of these cross-checks. For instance, it is impossible to give the correct report on output and the correct report on labor force and at the same time falsify the report on labor productivity. If the enterprise tried to support the falsified indicator of labor productivity by understating the number of persons employed, it would also have to falsify the report on the amount of wages paid out and so on in a never-ending chain of interrelated magnitudes. The first thing the superior organ does on receiving a report from an enterprise is to check it for internal consistency. In view of this close examination of internal consistency, the room for maneuver in falsifying reports is extremely limited. Another factor that makes it difficult to falsify reports is that the rules for drawing up statistical reports and for carrying out accounting are prescribed in minute detail from above.

The controls which the superior organ has over the enterprise are well illustrated by the position of the chief bookkeeper in the enterprise. In a number of respects the chief bookkeeper is not subject to the authority of the manager of the enterprise at all but to the superior organ. Many of the documents associated with transactions of the enterprise require his signature and he is not supposed to carry out the orders of the manager and indicate his approval if these transactions involve some illegality or falsification. He is officially described as the "eye of the state" within the enterprise, and the listing of his functions and responsibilities makes it clear that he is to insure accurate reporting to his boss, the bookkeeping department of the superior organ. Even so, the superior organ does not really trust the reports presented by the enterprise and it is envisaged in Soviet accounting legislation that an auditor from the central organization will audit the books of every enterprise once a year.

It should not be concluded from all that we have said that reports submitted by Soviet enterprises are never falsified. Some kinds of falsification will get by and careful research into the kinds of falsification that enterprises try to carry off provides interesting insights into the nature of managerial behavior in the Soviet system. But the point is that falsification is a dangerous business and the distortions that one can safely get away with are likely to be relatively minor.

Moreover, the checks performed by the superior organ are only the beginning. There are many other chains of command and information that reach into the enterprise. One of the most important is the *Gosbank,* the "one big bank," which services the whole Soviet economy. It is in a particularly strategic position to check on and control enterprise actions since all the monetary transactions of the enterprise pass through its hands. Generally speaking, Soviet enterprises use very little cash in their transactions. They sell their output to other state organizations and are paid by transfers of bank balances rather than by the exchange of actual cash. Thus the Soviet firm never has much access to cash and makes payments from its bank account by writing orders to the bank authorizing transfers. One of the main functions entrusted to the bank is the duty of checking on the legality of these transactions. Prices must be in accordance with prices fixed by the government, payments must be for purposes specified in the plan, and so on. The one transaction for which the enterprise draws cash from the bank is for payment of its workers and in this case the bank is supposed to exercise particularly careful control. The bank does not simply hand over whatever money the enterprise says it needs to pay workers but checks wage payments against the plan and checks the payroll, including the names of payees, to make certain that they are really employed in the enterprise.

The Ministry of Finance, the Central Statistical Administration, and the Committee on State Security are three more control agencies. Each of these has some responsibility for checking on the reports of enterprises and all of them have auditing staffs which have access to the books of an individual enterprise. In practice, of course, there are many deficiencies in the work of all these controllers. The workers in the bank may forego any careful control over the enterprise, enterprises may go unaudited for long periods of time, and the auditing may be done very carelessly. Altogether, the system of control agencies works with much less than ideal perfection.

Finally, two very important channels of communication and agencies for control are the Communist Party and the secret police. The Communist Party is organized in a structure which parallels the whole administrative structure of the Soviet economy. In every unit of the economy is a representative, and perhaps an organization of the Communist Party, which constitutes a separate channel of communication into the work and life of that economic unit. In many plants of strategic importance the secret police may actually have offices located right in the enterprise and in many other cases, of course, a less formalized system of informers and representatives exists.

This may seem like an excessively complicated set of controllers to post as watchdogs over the activities of economic units. But it is one of the essential mechanisms required to prevent bureaucratic degeneracy. In a system like the Soviet economy, there is very great pressure applied from above to show big achievements. The increases in output, the improvements in efficiency, the cost reductions — all of which those at the top of the pyramid of authority demand relentlessly — require great effort and initiative on the part of lower-level managers, especially in view of some of the adverse circumstances hampering the work of a manager in the Soviet economy. As a result of this great pressure, there is always a danger that people at the lower level, *including the controllers,* will form a coalition against pressure from above. For instance, life is really much easier for the chairman of an economic council if he can report that all the plants in his jurisdiction are working wonderfully well, increasing output, cutting costs, and reducing labor requirements. And if enterprises propose relatively easy plans from below, it may be to the interest of the economic council not to act the relentless task master but simply to approve the easy plans and defend them as they pass on up the hierarchy. Similarly, if the Party group within a plant knows that there are unexploited possibilities for increasing output, or even that certain illegal operations are being carried out, it may prefer to remain quiet about such deficiencies so long as every one else thinks the plant is doing the best it possibly can. If the local Party officials report that the managers in its territory are getting away with something, those on top might consider this the fault of the local Party officials. The Russians have a special term — "familyness" (*semeistvennost'*) — for this phenomenon of collusion among the controllers and the controlled. It constitutes a potential weakness in any bureaucratic structure and the Soviet regime takes great pains to fight it. For instance, it shifts persons from one position to another fairly often to break the ties that might otherwise be built up, and the multiplicity of lines of communication and control which we have just described involves a widening of the circle of persons who would have to be drawn into such a coalition. The existence of multiple channels of communication along which information can flow upward and pressure be exerted from the top makes more difficult the establishment of the family conspiracy.

The Measurement of Success.　The second big problem in operating this system of incentives involves the choice of appropriate indicators of plan fulfillment. The Russians have a more difficult problem here than American corporations generally do. The American corporation can usually rely on profit as the main criterion for evaluating the performance of the managers of subunits within the corporation. Profit provides a single general index in which all aspects of economic performance are more or less appropriately reflected. As long as the prices underlying the profit calculation are more or less accurate reflectors of wants and sacrifices in the national economy as a whole, profit is an appropriate criterion for judging how well the firm is satisfying its social role of producing economically what is needed.

In the Soviet economy, however, the higher level of administrative officials are not able safely to rely on profit as the most important indicator for evaluating the performance of enterprise directors. Because of distortions in the price system (see below), maximizing profit at the level of the enterprise does not mean maximizing the overall objectives of the regime. Frequently prices are set below cost on certain very badly needed items, while other, less crucially needed items may have prices which allow high profits. If, in such a situation, managers were told that their performance would be judged on the basis of their profits, disequilibrium between supplies and demands would develop quickly. The unreliability of profit as an index of the best action from the point of view of the national economy forces the planners to specify in considerable detail just how enterprise management should operate; the plan which an enterprise receives in the Soviet economy specifies not a single goal but many separate ones. At the very minimum, the plan will indicate the size of the labor force and the volume of wage payments, the amounts of various kinds of materials that will be allocated to the enterprise, a cost budget, the total value of output, and the amount of profit that is to be earned. In most industries the plan will specify a number of indicators in addition to these. These details cannot be left to the discretion of the enterprise director because they have been painstakingly fitted into the overall system of plans beforehand. Encouraging management to disregard them in favor of maximizing profit would cause endless trouble.

The fact that so many details are laid down complicates the job of the superior organ when it comes to evaluate the fulfillment of the plan as a whole. Plans are never so accurate or the manager's control over his operations so complete that he will just fulfill all the indicators exactly. It usually happens that he will do better than the plan on some of the targets but underfill some others, or at least meet different targets in varying degrees. When this happens, a perplexing problem of evaluation arises for the authorities. What should their reaction be if the output plan has been overfulfilled by 10 per cent but the planned wages expenditure has been exceeded by 5 per cent or if the plant has produced 20 per cent more of one commodity than the plan specified but 10 per cent less than the planned amount of another? How can these various indexes of performance be balanced off against one another so that it is possible to decide whether or not the plan has been fulfilled and whether or not to hand out rewards or to employ sanctions for failure? Clearly what happens in such a situation is that sooner or later there must emerge some set of priorities which guide the controllers in making their evaluations of plan fulfillment. And once the managers have learned what the trade-off between the relative importance of different indicators is, they will adjust their behavior accordingly.

The establishment of the correct system of priorities is a tricky business, however. Whenever controllers give high priority to one particular goal in their evaluation of plan fulfillment and make that priority effective through bonuses, enterprise managers will violate other parts of the plan in order to fulfill the high priority indicator. For instance, when the machine tractor stations (MTS) were still in operation,[1] one of their important success indicators

---

[1] The machine tractor stations were state organizations which until recently owned most of the agricultural machinery of the country and did work for the collective farms for a share of the output of the collective farm. They have now been liquidated and their machinery sold to the collective farms.

was reduction of fuel expenditure in tractor work. Fuel is one of the biggest inputs into tractor operation and naturally the controllers wanted to motivate people to reduce fuel expenditure. But because of the high priority of this goal, the managers of MTS did many things that were clearly undesirable and irrational in order to improve this one indicator and get bonuses. They would systematically plow to less than the standard depth, refuse to do for the collective farms those kinds of work that required more fuel, and in other ways interfere with effective work of the collective farms.

Another interesting illustration of the principle occurred in the electric power industry. Electric power stations themselves consume a certain fraction of the power they produce to run various kinds of machinery in the power station. In the Soviet Union this internal consumption has been higher than it should be by, say, comparison with United States plants. The authorities made reduction in internal consumption a high-priority goal and bonuses were given for good performance with regard to this indicator. The reaction of managers of electric power plants was rational enough from their own point of view. Disregarding any calculations about which was cheapest, they scrapped electric motors used to drive their equipment and replaced them with steam and internal combustion engines. But of course such a substitution was not really efficient for the economy as a whole and was not intended when the bonuses for reduction of internal consumption were established. Installation of new machinery involved a waste of investment funds and its operation meant some increase in costs, but since the system of priorities did not place much emphasis on these indicators, the waste was overlooked and managers got their bonuses for being wasteful!

There is a difficult problem even in defining the measure by which any one of the many goals specified in the plan is evaluated. The most important indicator in the plan has always been the volume of output but the ambiguities inherent in measuring the volume of output frequently lead to thoroughly irrational behavior. The output of any enterprise is likely to be heterogeneous, that is, it consists of many different kinds of output. Even if its output seems to be essentially one kind of thing, steel, for example, a simple physical measure of its volume is likely to ignore important economic dimensions of the product — such as quality or degree of fabrication. Thus, to define it in one way means that the other dimensions can be neglected by the enterprise in its drive to fulfill the output target. When window glass output was measured in tons, it was advantageous for the enterprise to make glass extra thick — which meant saving on processing and handling. But of course from the point of view of the national economy, this meant a reduction in the area that could be covered with a given tonnage of glass. When the measure of output was redefined as an areal one, i.e., square meters of glass produced, the enterprise found it advantageous to make glass extra thin. The enterprise effort to do what seemed advantageous to itself meant a waste of resources for the economy as a whole — a Soviet discussion of the problem said that one-fourth of all glass arriving at construction sites was broken and the author blamed this on the excessive thinness of the glass.

The most generally used measure of output in Soviet industry has always been *valovaia produktsiia,* or value of gross output. Since the controllers are especially interested in growth, this indicator has been defined in terms of constant prices so that it can measure increases in physical volume from period to period. As a gross rather than a net measure of output, it includes the value of purchased materials consumed as well as the value added in the enterprise in question. These two circumstances have caused all kinds of trouble. For instance, because the measure is gross output, there is a temptation for the manager to fulfill his output plan by emphasizing those products which are "material intensive," products which have large inputs of purchased materials and parts per unit of output. The main bottleneck which the manager faces in achieving the output goal is his limited labor supply and the limited processing capacity of his enterprise. If he spreads this labor and processing capacity over a larger volume of raw materials, he naturally gets a larger gross output, although the net value his enterprise has added is no different in either case. Thus managers try to minimize production of commodities that require little raw material and much processing in favor of material-intensive products.

The use of constant prices to measure output frequently stimulates the enterprise to violate the assigned assortment of output. As the economy grows and becomes more productive, costs of production (or, in other words, real inputs into commodities) change very unevenly. The cost of production of some commodities falls much faster than the cost of others. So it frequently happens that commodities which have high prices in the base year from which the constant prices are taken experience rapid reductions in costs but for other commodities this does not happen. Faced with limited allocations of materials and limited processing capacity and labor, the manager finds it easier to fulfill his output plan by producing large amounts of the high-value commodities which take relatively small amounts of inputs. The others he neglects. Thus there may arise consistent shortages of some goods, excesses of others. The difficulty of finding an unambiguous measure of performance arises for other indicators as well, such as cost. One interesting case involved the goal for costs of production in book publishing. Clearly if the plan specified simply cost per book the enterprise would be tempted to produce only small books and to print these in large editions. So the planners instead specified the cost plan in terms of cost per printed page. What the book publishers did then was to use larger type, to put wider margins on the pages, and more space between the lines. One of the biggest costs in book publishing is the editorial and typesetting work, and if this is spread over a larger and larger number of pages, there is naturally a reduction in the cost per page. So this indicator had exactly the opposite effect from what was intended. It tempted the book publishers to seek success and earn bonuses by wasting paper and binding materials, rather than by reducing costs and making savings. Very often these problems can be solved by changing the indicator or by changing the system of priorities, though solving one problem this way often means creating a new one, as in the book publishing case above.

It would be wrong to overemphasize these difficulties in the motivation and controlling system. The examples we have discussed are characteristic diseases to which the Soviet system is subject but it manages to survive them. A considered judgment would probably be that the Soviet regime has managed to motivate and control its managerial elite fairly effectively. The material rewards offered for successful performance are great enough to elicit an adequate supply of effort and talent. At the same time the system of control has been arranged so that managers must really perform in order to win these awards. This is not to say that the system works perfectly. There are ways of evading responsibility; certain aspects of the control system encourage people to engage in actions that are irrational from the national economic point of view; and the operation of the system of checks and controls represents a considerable overhead cost for the economy. Until recently, however, the wastes and inefficiencies arising from imperfections in the control system were probably outweighed by the kind of pressure for growth which this system of crude commands and evaluations enabled the leaders to exert on production enterprises. Whether this judgment can remain valid for the future is more problematical. The main problem is essentially one of getting enough information and being able to handle it. The difficulties we have described arise because the controllers — through lack of time, understanding or capacity for handling and absorbing detail — have had to assess the performance of enterprises on the basis of too few and overly simple indicators. More sophisticated methods of evaluation depend on having more information about all aspects of the enterprise's operation but, given the crude technology of data handling (with the abacus and pen and ink as the main technical aids), the low level of economic sophistication, and the ambivalence of motivations in the hierarchy, it would have been very difficult and expensive to get more information. And of course this problem is growing all the time. As production relationships become more complicated, interdependence among different units more complex, and the information problem more and more difficult, the cost of these imperfections becomes much greater. This is one of the underlying issues in the current concern about either increasing radically the information handling capacity of the system or delegating more authority and choice to the enterprise level and simplifying the measurement of success by more reliance on profit as a comprehensive indicator.

The Soviet Price System.   One obstacle to rational decision making common to all these problems, and to many others as well, is the Soviet price system. Decision making always involves weighing one set of considerations against another. The questions take the form of — "Is the extra output worth the extra cost?" "Is the saving in the future worth the extra cost right now?" "Is the cost of this way of doing something more or less than the cost of doing it some other way?" The function of prices is to reduce all the considerations on each side to a single number, representing the cost or value, so that we can tell which way is cheapest or whether the value of the output equals or exceeds the cost. In deciding whether it is best to dieselize or electrify a given section of railway line, for example, the alternatives involve very different combinations of inputs and, in order to see which is cheapest, we have to aggregate these by means of prices. If prices are not a fairly accurate reflection of the real burden to the economy of producing these alternative combinations, then there is a danger that decision makers will choose the alternatives that look cheapest on paper but are not cheapest in reality. Similarly, if the prices to which the *khozraschet* decision maker refers in deciding what is most advantageous for him in terms of the established success indicators depart very far from the real value of output or the real costs on inputs, then the pursuit of his local interest will be wasteful of resources from the overall point of view.

The Soviet price system does indeed seem to be a very imperfect measure of the real costs of resources. In the Soviet Union prices are set not by a process of supply and demand but by administrative order. Most prices are set by fairly high-level organs of government, others by price-setting organs in the ministries or the economic councils, and some are set by local authorities. The point of departure for setting most prices is supposed to be the reported cost of production but, in practice, prices have usually departed considerably from the actual costs of production. The prices of some goods reflect large subsidies, while others have been set high enough to return very high rates of profit. Moreover, the prices customarily do not include any charges for rent or capital and seldom reflect the use value to the customer. Once set, prices have remained fixed for long periods of time. This is an important administrative convenience for the planners in making their many different kinds of calculations and drawing up plans but it means that, as costs change with the passage of time, prices get out of line with costs. As a result of these peculiarities in the planners' accounting and pricing system, the price placed on a good has often been an inaccurate measure of what it really cost to produce it or what it was worth.

With such distortions in the price system, it is very difficult for planners to know whether their choice of the cheapest way of doing something is in reality correct. Soviet planners themselves have frequently expressed doubts about the validity of calculations based on existing prices. In many cases they have tried to make unofficial corrections of existing prices to render them more nearly accurate measures of real cost to the national economy but such guesswork corrections are likely to be arbitrary and inaccurate. Because the Russians, as Marxists, did not appreciate the function of prices or understand the correct principles of price determination, they never quite understood how to reform them properly. More recently, their new sophistication in the understanding of value and allocation has changed this situation on the analytical level, though as of 1965 they still had not gone very far in actually reforming the price system to make it an accurate guide to decision making. We will return in the final chapter to this issue of the recent advances which the Russians have made in understanding the concept of value and the proper principles of price formation.

5

The Command Principle vs. the Market Approach

Central planning and the command principle are simply incapable of handling certain aspects of the problem of allocation, as was suggested in Chapter 3, and in some areas of the Soviet economy the regime has found it expedient to rely to a considerable extent on the market mechanism — for instance, in the allocation of labor and the allocation of consumer goods. The same considerations that have induced the regime to rely on market techniques in these two areas are important in some other areas as well, especially in agriculture and foreign trade. In the latter cases, however, the Russians have not been willing to trust market methods of allocation and the explanation for this different outcome is instructive. Analysis of this difference in approach leads directly to the question of the virtues and failings of the Soviet command technique of resource allocation compared with the market approach, and the last section of the chapter reviews Soviet planning from that point of view.

The Labor and Consumer Goods Markets

In its relationship with the population, the Soviet regime is in a position similar to that of the single employer in a company town.

It owns all the property or "means of production" but, in order to operate this production establishment, it has to call on the population for labor. In order to maintain the population and to provide incentives it must also devote part of the output of the economy to the support of households. It sells back part of the output to them through the company store. In this relationship there is an illuminating contrast with the methods used for allocating resources and making decisions *within* the production establishment which have been discussed in the two preceding chapters. The general approach for running the internal affairs of the company is to rely on the command principle — the bosses tell each unit, such as a steel mill, what inputs to use, what technical policies to follow, how many laborers it may hire, to whom it should ship its output. The difficulty of trying to apply this same principle to the approximately 100 million persons in the Soviet labor force is obvious. It is as if each person in a company town were told what occupation to enter, what skills to acquire, where to work, and, on the other side, were allocated a set of supporting inputs — a specified ration of consumption items. Any attempt to do this would be impossibly cumbersome and inefficient. There are simply too many people involved and they are too differentiated from each other in the relevant respects, i.e., in their tastes and talents. The productivity of an economy must depend to a considerable extent on the motivation of workers. Unless the worker brings to his job a measure of skill, some pride in his work, and a willingness to learn, the capacity of the economy to produce and progress must surely suffer. Given the tremendous variations in human personality and in the requirements of different jobs, one important element in getting the most out of the labor force is to get the right man connected with the right job. Another is to suit the reward (primarily material) which he earns to his special tastes and circumstances. Because people's tastes are so different, the amount of effort that can be gotten out of the labor force will be much less if we simply pay each worker a standard ration than if we allow each to choose the particular market basket of goods and services that he considers best. The best approach to both these problems would seem to be to let households make their own choices, guiding and controlling them through the use of a price system. A price system has been defined as "the terms on which alternatives are offered." By setting prices on consumer goods and on various kinds and grades of labor, the Soviet regime is telling households the terms on which it will deal with them. "If you want to be a janitor, you can expect X rubles of income; but if you have the talent and are willing to make the effort and acquire the training to become an engineer and thereby make a bigger contribution to productivity, we are prepared to pay you a much bigger income." At the same time it is communicating to them by the prices it has set on consumer goods the manifold combinations of goods into which they can translate that ruble income. This approach will secure much more effort from the labor force than the system applied in a military organization or on a slave plantation which simply assigns a person to a job and doles out the standard ration. Thus even under socialist planning it has been found expedient to organize the link with households in two more or less free markets — a consumer goods market and a labor market. Reliance on the market and on the price system to guide decisions in this area imposes a certain discipline however. The terms offered, i.e., the relative prices on consumer goods and the wage structure, must satisfy certain conditions if the method is to be effective and if the resulting allocation is to be rational.

Financial Equilibrium. The first condition is that the general level of prices in these two markets relative to each other be set so as to achieve macro-balance. The total amount paid out as wages through the labor market must be just sufficient to buy back the consumer goods offered in the other market. Consider the following simplified model of an economy. Suppose that the Gosplan plans to produce 100 billion rubles worth of output, of which it proposes to allocate 60 billion rubles for household consumption, with the other 40 billion planned to be used for various state objectives such as investment or military spending. A moment's thought makes it clear that the creation of 100 billion rubles worth of goods means paying out to workers money incomes of 100 billion rubles. What makes the aggregate output worth 100 billion rubles is the fact that it has cost 100 billion rubles to produce it and in the Soviet economy the only primary resource for which compensation is paid is labor.[1] There are no interest or rent payments of any significance. Obviously there is going to be something wrong in this situation. The population will have 100 billion rubles with which to buy 60 billion rubles worth of goods and the state will have nothing with which to pay for the 40 billion rubles worth of investment goods which the planners have caused to be produced for it.

The state could simply create additional money to pay for the investment goods, leaving the population with the 100 billion rubles to spend on 60 billion rubles worth of goods. But that would not be at all a satisfactory solution. It is true that under the system of physical plans consumers could not divert additional resources into consumer goods production by bidding up consumer goods prices and making them more profitable. But the excess purchasing power would have a disastrous effect on incentives. There would be no point in going back to the factory to earn more money if one already had money which could not be spent for anything. Thus the physical division of the output of the economy into consumption goods and investment goods must somehow be re-inforced by a system of financial controls which absorbs the excess purchasing power and assures financial equilibrium. Somehow 40 billion rubles of the income received by the population will have to be taken away from them and given to the state to use in paying enterprises for the 40 billion rubles worth of investment goods. The answer obviously is some kind of tax. An income tax would have adverse effects on morale. Marginal rates of taxation would have to be so high that people might be discouraged from asking the extra effort to produce more or to increase their skills. The regime has worked hard to create the incentive system and it would not make sense to dilute it by too obvious a tax bite. An income tax would be an obvious kind of exploitation that people would resent.

The technique which Soviet planners have found most satis-factory for mopping up the excess purchasing power is an indirect, invisible tax, the famous "turnover tax." The price which the

---

[1] It is true that any production enterprise as one of its costs will have payments to other enterprises for materials. But eventually this outlay ends up as wages to the workers of the supplying enterprises or other workers still further back in the chain of suppliers.

producer of consumer goods receives is sufficient only to cover his costs and to give him a small profit. In the wholesale distribution network, however, a heavy tax is placed on consumer goods, so that when these goods reach the retailers they are priced at levels far above their costs. The price paid by the consumer is nearly twice the cost of producing and distributing the goods, with the difference accounted for by the turnover tax. Until recently not much more than half the money paid by the population for consumer goods went to pay the costs of producing and distributing them — the rest was tax. In the last several years, this method of collecting the excess purchasing power has given way in some degree to another method, i.e., setting wholesale prices throughout the economy high enough to generate large profits. (When the prices are fixed by the state, obviously it makes little difference whether we call the spread between cost and price a profit or a tax.) But even in 1963, turnover tax collections, nearly all collected on consumer goods, amounted to a little over one-third of the value of retail sales of consumer goods to the population.

Micro-balance — Clearing Individual Markets. Effective use of markets in dealing with households also imposes a necessity for "micro-balance." Relative prices must be set to clear individual markets — they must be juggled to ensure equality of supply and demand for each consumer good and for all the different categories of labor. It would be undesirable to have the prices on shoes so low that there was a shortage of shoes and the prices of television sets so high that the available supply could not be sold. Such disequilibria in the consumer goods markets are wasteful of people's time, produce frustration, and, even worse, create the conditions for speculation and black markets. When there are shortages, people spend too much time standing in line, they cannot find the goods they want, and one who succeeds in getting hold of scarce goods can resell them at a large profit to someone else who did not. Such uncontrolled activities and the incomes to which they give rise have always been seen by the Soviet regime as very threatening. Surpluses, on the other hand, are a clear waste from the point of view of the regime — resources tied up in unsalable television sets certainly are not making any contribution toward extracting effort from the population. The same desiderata apply in the labor market — the planners would not want to find that the existing wage pattern failed to attract enough people into some occupation such as that of bookkeeper, foreman, or nurse, or that it offered insufficient incentive to move people into whatever new projects or new regions they were trying to open up.

Consumer Sovereignty. The requirement of clearing the market is obvious and easy enough to understand — whenever it is not met, the problems of shortages and surpluses emerge immediately. This is not to say that the Russians have usually succeeded in achieving micro-balance, but failure to do so leads to obviously undesirable results that the planners can appreciate. It takes no great sophistication for them to sense that shortages call for raising prices, excesses for lowering them. But if the resulting allocation is to satisfy the requirements of rational resource use from the point of view of the Soviet planners, another more subtle and less obvious condition must also be satisfied.

Price relationships among consumer goods should be the same as their cost relationships. If a suit costs three times as much to produce as a pair of shoes, the prices at which they are sold to the population should be in that same ratio. This rule says that the rate at which turnover tax is charged on consumer goods should be the same for every good. Prices on goods sold to the population will be considerably above what it actually costs to produce them (to solve the macro-balance problem), but the ratio of price to cost should be the same for each good. In the example above, where goods costing 60 billion rubles are to be sold at 100 billion rubles, each good should be priced at $1\frac{2}{3}$ its cost. The reasoning behind this principle can be understood from the following figures.

	Shoes	Peanut Butter	Shoes and Peanut Butter
Number of units sold	2,000 pairs	4,000 kilos	
Actual cost per unit	15 rubles/pair	5 rubles/kilo	
Turnover tax	15 " "	10 " "	
Selling price per unit	30 " "	15 " "	
Aggregate value	$30 \times 2,000 = 60,000$	$15 \times 4,000 = 60,000$	120,000

Imagine that these are the only consumer goods there are and that both macro-balance and micro-balance have been achieved. That is, at these prices, demand just equals supply for each good, and the aggregate value of the goods of 120,000 rubles just exhausts the purchasing power that has been handed out in wages. The resulting allocation would still be wasteful. Consider the effect of reducing the production of shoes and increasing the production of peanut butter. Given the relative prices, decreasing shoe production and sales by one pair would mean a loss of revenue of 30 rubles. To maintain macro-balance, that 30 rubles would have to be made up by producing and selling more peanut butter to the population — 2 kilos more, to be precise. But a look at the cost figures shows that this shift has saved the regime some resources. The cost of the extra peanut butter (resources worth 10 rubles) was more than covered by the saving of resources in shoe production (15 rubles worth) and the regime has saved itself 5 rubles worth of resources which can now be devoted to some goal of the regime such as investment or military spending. And the important point is that this gain was made without diminishing the welfare of the population. Their behavior shows that they are just as well satisfied as before. They were perfectly willing to give up one pair of shoes to get two kilos of peanut butter. As this shift continued, of course, the "market clearing price" for peanut butter would have to come down and that for shoes rise, by lowering the rate of turnover tax in the one case and raising it in the other. The advantage of further shifts would vanish just at the point we have suggested, i.e., where the ratio of price to cost is just equal for both goods. This conclusion can also be stated in terms of the concept of consumers' sovereignty. We said earlier that we take for granted that in general the choice of what resources ought to be used for in the Soviet-type economy is the prerogative of the regime, not of the population. But the example shows that within the limits of the amount of resources allocated for the satisfaction of consumer wants, consumer sovereignty should rule. This is necessary in order to minimize the volume of resources devoted to consumption and hence to permit the regime to maximize the attainment of its own goals.

The analogue of this principle in the labor market is that not only must prices just equate the supply of each category of labor with the requirement for that kind of labor but they must also be proportional to the productivity of different workers. Raising pay to whatever level is required to attract enough workers to man the coal mines of Vorkuta does not by itself guarantee efficiency — it might turn out that the wage rate that would have to be paid was so high that the cost of the coal would be excessive compared to other ways of meeting the fuel needs satisfied by Vorkuta coal. Just as in the case of the consumer goods market, rationality through the market approach requires adjustment in the quantities of different categories of labor demanded until the market clearing prices are proportioned to the contribution that each worker makes toward production, as well as to the relative attractiveness of different jobs in his estimation.

What has been said so far is essentially theoretical — an exercise in the application of the theory of markets. The question naturally arises of how well the Soviet approach to the labor market and the consumer goods market conforms in practice to these requirements for rationality. The answer is complex. In the first two decades of their history the Russians did a very poor job of achieving macrobalance and suffered from inflation as a consequence. Money incomes of the population always exceeded planned amounts and this surplus purchasing power was not immediately extracted. The regime, therefore, had constantly to be raising prices of consumer goods to get rid of the unplanned increases in purchasing power. At the same time, the rise in wage payments forced up costs in most enterprises and the government had to increase wholesale prices on producers' goods as well so that enterprises could cover their costs. This inflation led to many difficulties in planning and administration of the economy. Changing price levels and changing relationships between physical goods and value magnitudes are bound to complicate planning and control. More recently, since about 1950, financial planning and financial controls have greatly improved and the Soviet economy has managed to prevent inflation and even achieve some deflation of the general price level. But the most interesting thing about the experience of the thirties is that slackness in financial controls did not frustrate the channeling of a large portion of the national income into investment. The system of physical controls described earlier made that possible even when financial equilibrium was not attained.

This point deserves special emphasis. The high rate of investment and the correspondingly rapid rate of growth of the Soviet economy come from the tight control over resources which the planners possess, rather than from the virtues of planning as such. In any industrialization program an increase in investment is one of the crucial factors and one in which industrialization programs of underdeveloped countries may fail if control over resource allocation is left with households. As soon as incomes begin to increase, people try to spend these incomes for consumption rather than saving them to finance further investment. This causes no end of trouble. The competition for resources may cause an inflation or the increase in incomes may be spent for imported goods which leads to foreign exchange difficulties. To the extent that any increase in output comes first in agriculture, the rural population is likely to eat up this increase rather than leaving it as a surplus. There are difficulties then in providing a food supply for a growing nonindustrial labor force which could add to the national output by virtue of various kinds of productive activity in the cities. Soviet planning has found an effective way of limiting consumption in real terms but has not found a way of eliminating sacrifice. This is a feature of the Soviet industrialization model which its potential emulators should ponder carefully.

Nor have the Russians honored the micro-balance requirements very consistently. At various times they have injected a considerable degree of administrative interference into both the consumer goods market and the labor market. They have resorted to rationing in the consumer goods market over an appreciable part of their history and have used administrative controls and criminal sanctions as a substitute for wage incentives in the labor market. Beginning in the late thirties, the Russians tried increasingly to put people in jobs and to make them work by means of coercive labor controls in lieu of wage incentives. Workers were more or less tied to their jobs by means of labor booklets. The labor booklet was a permanent work record which the worker had to surrender to his employer on getting a job. He could not get a new job without surrendering the labor booklet and unless his employer was willing to release him by returning the labor booklet, he could not move to another job. During this period the law also provided severe punishments for workers who were late for work, who came to work drunk, or were absent from work. At one point a worker who was twenty minutes late for work might end up with a prison sentence of two to four months.

Over time the Russians have generally moved more and more toward reliance on market principles and away from administrative direction in both these markets. In the labor market especially after 1956, there was a big effort to dismantle the coercive labor controls instituted during the war and to reform the wage system so as to satisfy the micro-balance requirements described above. In the consumer goods market the Russians have generally preferred to avoid the clumsiness and costs of rationing, though their pricing has never been flexible enough to keep supply and demand nicely in equilibrium. The consequences of this failure — shortages and surpluses — are there for all to see and the remedy is not hard to figure out.

On the other hand, the Russians have not been good enough economists to see that it is in the interests of the regime to honor consumers' sovereignty within the limits of resources allocated to consumption. And, as a matter of fact, the Russians have been much more likely to seek micro-balance in consumer goods markets by juggling turnover tax rates and prices on consumer goods than by adjusting quantities to conform to consumer preferences. This is understandable, both in terms of their failure to understand the issue at stake and in terms of the way production decisions get made. It will be remembered from the discussion of the two preceding chapters that determination of the mix of consumer goods is made in response to the exigencies of balancing and the pressures of *khozraschet* expediencies. The producers' motivation is to satisfy their bosses rather than to satisfy their customers.

An interesting development in the last several years has been the experimental introduction of a new system of motivations for producers of consumer goods and a new freedom for them to determine their outputs in accordance with what the retailers discover the public wants. Beginning in 1964, the Russians permitted the management in two plants to determine their own assortment mix and to settle on prices by negotiation with the merchandisers rather than with the central planners. The enterprise plan was specified in much less detail than formerly and the management was free within the general constraint of a specified output level and the goal of maximizing profits to respond to the retailers' desire for goods of higher quality, for new kinds of output, and for variations in style so that goods would be salable. The experiment was judged a success and during 1965 it was extended to a total of 400 enterprises in the apparel, textile, and leather industries. One can well imagine that this is not going to be a complete solution — there will surely come a point where the changes that a consumer goods factory needs to make to produce the goods that consumers want will involve a need for a different kind of machinery or a different kind of raw materials, say, chemical fibers of a certain kind or better materials for the tanning of leather. Here again there will be a confrontation between the part of the economy that is run by the command principle and that which is responsive to the needs of the buyer. At this interface the command principle will retain its hegemony and the industries producing consumer goods will be unable to adjust their activity in accordance with consumer wishes. But in general this new approach makes it feasible within fairly broad limits to alter the composition of consumer goods output rather than rationing out a predetermined market basket by juggling prices out of all relation to costs.

How well the wage structure conforms to the relative productivity of different kinds of labor is hard to say. But one would guess that it is easier for Soviet decision makers to be nudged in the right direction here by administrative considerations than it is in the consumer goods problem. Soviet discussions of wage setting show a considerable awareness of the importance of productivity considerations in setting relative wages; and, in general, enterprise management is freer to adjust the quantities of labor he hires to minimize costs under a given wage structure than consumer goods producers are to alter the mix or quality of consumer goods to produce what people want.

Agriculture

The above discussion provides a useful approach for interpreting some of the persistent problems the Russians have had in managing agriculture. Since agriculture is an important sector in its own right, it will be useful to make a detour here to describe some of its distinctive features and some of the things that make it different from other sectors, such as industry, on which the discussion has concentrated so far. We will then be ready for an interpretation of agricultural problems and policy in terms of the relative applicability of market versus administrative controls to agriculture.

Agricultural Organization.   There are three distinct economies in the Soviet agricultural sector — state farms (*sovkhozy*), collective farms (*kolkhozy*), and private production on the small plots which collective farm members and some other members of the population are permitted to farm on their own account. State farms are operated like any other state production establishment and their output is intended primarily for sale to state procurement agencies. There is a relatively small number of them (about 9,000 in 1963); they work with a hired labor force; and they are fairly well controlled by the mechanisms of planning and administration common elsewhere in the Soviet economy. State farms are more or less specialized in certain lines of agricultural production such as wheat farming, ranching and others.

Collective farms theoretically are cooperative enterprises managed and operated by and for the benefit of their members. In fact, central planning has placed many constraints on their autonomy and they have been exploited by the general techniques suggested in Chapter 2 to provide resources for accumulation. A very large portion of their output is required to be sold to the state. The money income thus earned, together with whatever output has not been sold, is distributed among the members in accordance with their productive contribution as measured in "labor-days." The various jobs are rated and the collective farmers' work recorded in this unit of account. A labor-day is not literally a day's labor — a day's labor at the more skilled or responsible jobs may be rated at more than one labor-day, at less for other jobs. The incentive effect of renumeration in labor-days has always been diluted by the fact that the collective farmer works for an uncertain share in a future pot of unknown size. More important, because the state requires so much of collective farm output and pays so low a price for it, the reward to collective farm members for working on the collective farms has generally been too low even to cover subsistence. Thus, for a large part of their income, collective farm members have had to rely on the output of small private plots which each collective farm household is permitted to have. These plots are small (usually somewhat over half an acre) but, by being cultivated intensively, they yield a considerable output which is either consumed as output in kind or turned into money income by sale on the collective farm market. The collective farm market is a more or less free market in which collective farmers sell surplus produce to the urban population at prices fixed essentially by supply and demand. Collective farmers and other citizens are also permitted to own specified numbers of livestock and in fact a large share of the farm animals in the U.S.S.R. is owned privately. In 1963, 42 per cent of all cows in the U.S.S.R., a third of the pigs, and most of the goats were owned privately. Thus the collective farm member is typically engaged in two kinds of activity at once — as a generally reluctant participant in collective farm production proper and in private farming on his own account. It has been estimated that approximately 44 per cent of all Soviet agricultural output originates in the collective operations of the collective farms, about 32 per cent on the private plots. The remaining quarter is the output of state farms.

Agriculture is a hybrid sector in terms of decision making and control. The three economies comprising it form a kind of continuum. State farms are at one end where the relatively small number of units, the use of traditional incentives, and the specialized character of the farms mean that the command principle characteristic of the rest of the economy can be more or less effectively used. At the other end, the central planners have scarcely attempted to influence decision making in private production. Though they have always tried to restrict and limit its interaction with the rest of the economy, the planners have left this activity almost completely outside the control of the command system. Its purpose is to enable the peasants to take care of their own subsistence and the planners have generally tried to levy fairly heavy tribute on it but generally speaking they do not try to enforce their decisions and make allocations in these operations.

In the middle of the spectrum is collective production in the *kolkhozy* which has been the dominant source for supplying what the modern industrial part of the economy requires in the way of food and agricultural raw materials. Here the situation is ambiguous — the planners have aspired to imposing on collective farm production the kind of central direction they use elsewhere. They issue commands about crop patterns, output goals; they allocate inputs; they try to centralize decision making. In the past, their agency for transmitting these commands was primarily the machine-tractor station and the procurement agencies. More recently it has been regional production boards. Also, throughout, one of the main functions of the local party apparatus has been to see that agricultural plans were carried out. Unfortunately, because of the large number of units, the variety of conditions in which they find themselves, the distance from the controllers, the obstacles which weather puts in the way of fixed routine, agriculture is just not a very promising sector for control by administrative techniques. It shares with household behavior some of the traits that make it desirable to rely on price to guide behavior.

Agricultural Performance. Performance in agriculture, and especially in this crucial middle part, has always been very poor. Collective farm agriculture is unreliable, irrational, wasteful, unprogressive — almost any pejorative adjective one can call to mind would be appropriate here. Much data to support this generalization will be considered in Chapters 6 and 7. The explanation lies in the inability of the Russians to cope with the basic dilemma described above. The objective conditions would seem to call for a kind of market approach toward agricultural production. The administrative approach has been feasible only in some special cases, as in the state farms. And there the administration found the serious disadvantage that the result was high costs, partly because they had to pay labor a living wage. On the other hand, it was not really possible to handle this link by a market approach. The point was made in Chapter 2 that the Soviet leaders concluded that they had to be exploitative, indeed confiscatory, to accumulate resources for industrialization but that it was much harder to do this in relation to agriculture than in relation to households. The administrators had a monopoly position in relation to urban households — to turn Marxist jargon against its users, the urban worker was alienated from the means of production, which were monopolized by the state. But the peasants were not equally dependent on the state and were harder to manipulate by the price nexus alone. The peasants had the land, the rain, and the sun, and were more nearly able to exist apart from the regime. The Stalinist formula for handling this dilemma was to use the administrative approach in a most coercive and dictatorial way. It did not work very well and led to an unstable situation. The failure of coercive administrative techniques called for more coercive methods — attacking the private plots, giving the machine tractor station power to dictate production decisions, arbitrarily forcing each region and each farm to deliver its share of the tribute required to meet the overall quotas. The latter disrupted proper regional specialization — everything had to be grown everywhere at whatever cost. The unwillingness of members to work in collective farm production was met with arbitrary requirements about the number of days that had to be worked by each member. Collective farm management in effect faced a fixed labor supply which in the accounting of the collective farm cost nothing except the meaningless labor-days, and so management had no incentive to economize on labor. It appears that toward the end of Stalin's reign the administration of agriculture simply followed the formula of making the pressure greater as things got worse.

Changes in Agriculture since Stalin. Stalin's heirs finally recognized that this was a self-defeating policy and have been engaged over the last fifteen years in an attempt to change the methods. The analysis above would suggest that market techniques might be a great help in getting effective use of resources and rational decision making in agriculture. The idea would be to post the prices, then let collective farms make their own decisions — about what crops to specialize in, what technology to use, whether to raise livestock or not — in response to prices. This indeed does seem to be the solution the Russians have been groping toward, albeit with some backsliding and some hesitation along the way. The abolition of the machine tractor stations and the transfer of machinery to the collective farms gave them a power of choice over machine use that they had never had before. There have been several reforms of the procurement prices at which the state buys collective farm output which have systematically led toward the principle of making these prices proportional to the cost of producing different kinds of output. One progressive move encouraged in the last few years is the paying of collective farm workers in cash rather than in the worthless labor-days. In some of his later speeches Khrushchev professed to foresee a day when the state would not even require deliveries from the collective farms — it would merely set prices based on the costs of the most efficient producers and let collective farms compete for the business. The idea is probably visionary at this stage but it shows a shrewd appreciation of the simplicity and desirability of confining the role of the state to setting prices and sloughing off the fruitless burden of administrative controls. This reorientation of policy has been founded on the gamble that the resulting improvements in incentives and productivity of resources will so increase output that the relationship with collective farmers need no longer be so exploitative. The gamble seems to have paid off. Real incomes have been made high enough so that, with a little administrative buttressing here and there, the price system proved a strong enough link to keep the collective farmers oriented toward the rest of the economy. Khrushchev's successors seem to have learned this lesson well and have gone even further to strengthen price incentives in controlling agriculture.

Agriculture has characteristically been a problem sector in all the Soviet-type economies and it is interesting that the policies followed recently in some of the East European economies strongly confirm the above analysis. In some of them, agriculture has been turned loose on a price tether more or less completely with quite successful results. Poland is the country which has gone farthest along these lines, even to the point of abandoning the collective farm. The result has been the most successful and productive agriculture of any Bloc country.

Foreign Trade

Foreign trade is not a very important aspect of the Soviet economy. It accounts for only a small per cent of Russian GNP and the U.S.S.R. is not one of the important traders in the world market. Nevertheless, the foreign trade sector is an interesting one to consider, both to illustrate the problem of choosing between the market approach and the command principle and to illuminate an important aspect of the relations among the various economies in the Soviet Bloc. For the Soviet-type economies in Eastern Europe, their small size makes foreign trade a great deal more significant in the total pattern of resource allocation and decision making than it is in the U.S.S.R. Foreign trade thus warrants more space and attention than its relative insignificance in the Soviet economy might indicate.

The volume of Soviet foreign trade is small relative to what might be expected in a country with a GNP the size of Russia's. In the early years of their industrialization drive, the Russians used foreign trade to help them evade some bottlenecks to growth. In the early thirties it was substantial but it then declined rapidly. In the postwar period there has been much talk by Soviet leaders of their interest in foreign trade and it has grown appreciably more rapidly than GNP. But given the size of its economy, the Soviet Union probably ought to trade much more than it does. The failure to trade more can be explained partly by the political motive to be independent of the capitalist countries and partly by a failure to appreciate fully the benefits of trade. But it must also be attributed partly to the fact that foreign trade is a very difficult activity to handle by the command principle. The relevant commands are essentially targets for imports and exports of various commodities issued to the foreign trade sector and analogous to the output and input targets worked out in the balancing process for any other sector. The foreign trade sector, however, has some distinctive features complicating its integration into this balancing process. First, it has nothing which resembles very closely the capacity measure that sets a limit to how much steel can be produced at the moment. Second, there is little restriction on the kind of goods that foreign trade might be asked to supply the domestic economy. Foreign trade offers the possibility of shopping in a world-wide supermarket. Even if we suppose that these two questions are settled somehow, the next step in the balancing process is for the sector to respond with a statement of its input requirements — in this case the quantities of goods to be allocated to the foreign trade people to be exported to pay for the imports. Lacking the kind of technological fixity that enables all other sectors to determine input requirements, the foreign trade ministry will have to reply that to produce (via foreign trade) the outputs requested it could use innumerable alternative combinations of exports. They could get rid of almost anything somewhere in the world at some price.

Foreign trade exasperates the central planners because of this kind of ambiguity and they are likely to use it only as a last resort. They are most likely to turn to foreign trade only when they discover some shortage for which they can find no other solution and are likely to offer the foreign trade sector as possible exports primarily such surpluses as happen to turn up in the balancing process. Given the general overcommitment of resources, the central balancers are likely to be much more keenly aware of the desirability of imports than of exports. It is most unlikely that they will want to give very high priority to investment requests to build up capacity beyond domestic needs for export purposes. These considerations are likely to mean that choices about what goods to export and import will be somewhat haphazard and seldom tested against the criterion of comparative advantage.

This problem is immensely magnified, of course, when two such countries try to deal with each other. The foreign trade planners of two such economies are likely to have a very hard time making deals. Each is free to buy and sell only what his central planners have allocated and there is little reason to expect that the list of things that one side needs to dispose of coincides with the list of things the other has been told to buy.

There is a striking similarity between this problem and dealing with agriculture and households. Decision making in foreign trade is done poorly because the range of choice is so wide and the interactions so complex. The issue is whether it might not be possible to ease bottlenecks by releasing some output to the foreign traders, in return for which they will get back enough of something in even tighter supply to lessen the overall pressure on the economy. But the number of relationships on which one has to have information and which one needs to consider to answer this question is simply too much for the Russians to handle. The central planners then must shrug their shoulders and forget about it or make wild guesses. Perhaps the market technique could well be used here to handle this sphere of choice more cheaply and effectively. The foreign trade ministry might be offered terms like those made to households. "We will take whatever you import and let you choose whatever output you need for export purposes. Where and what to buy and sell, how much and in what variety we leave entirely to you. But we set the prices and you will have to be financially independent. The principle you should follow is to look for every possible export-import combination that will pay for itself. That is, you should look systematically for something you can export that will earn enough foreign currency to enable you to import something that you can sell to us for more than you paid for the export." This is a perfectly sensible rule under one condition — that the prices posted are rational ones — and rationality here implies the same principles enunciated for the household link. The prices on export goods should be proportional to real costs (like the prices on consumer goods) and those offered for imports should reflect what they are worth in terms of productivity (like the wage rates).

This is the stumbling block, of course — the Russians have never dared trust their prices that far. And, given its large size, the Russian economy suffers less obvious loss from poor decision making in foreign trade than some smaller country might. It has the diversity of resources within its borders and large enough markets to assure production on an efficient scale, even if it sells only domestically. The smaller countries of East Europe stand to lose much more. As a result, they have been prompted to take some fairly bold steps in the direction of giving this kind of autonomy to foreign trade actors and reforming the price system to ensure that the resulting decisions are rational. One suspects that this experimentation with price and market principles in foreign trade has already been a big influence in getting them to decentralize and to think about prices and markets throughout the economy. The Soviet Union is likely to follow this lead much more slowly: Russian economists are too far from an understanding of the issues and the price system is too chaotic. Furthermore, in an economy this size the losses from irrational trade are likely to be small enough to be tolerable.

The unwillingness of the Russians to put foreign trade on this kind of a regimen is reflected in their approach to economic integration within the Bloc. They appreciate that there are potential gains from a more rational division of labor and more trade within the Bloc. But their proposal for achieving this is an extension of the traditional balancing process to a Bloc-wide territory. They have hoped for a supranational planning body that would use the same balancing techniques described in Chapter 3 to balance supply and demand for all commodities in the Bloc. They would not worry whether steel output matched the demand within the borders of any one country but only within the Bloc as a whole. There might be imbalances within any country but an overall balance for each commodity would mean that the surpluses of some countries would just equal the deficits of others. Foreign trade would be a by-product of balancing, just as interregional trade is within the borders of the Soviet Union. The Eastern European countries are apprehensive of a possible loss of control over their own economies under such an arrangement and the question of how to get rational specialization and foreign trade within the Bloc remains a controversial one.

Strengths and Weaknesses of Soviet Planning

Looking back over the last three chapters, we may now attempt an evaluation and interpretation of Soviet planning as a method of economic decision making and resource allocation. What sort of rating does it deserve with respect to its ability to make rational, efficient decisions about resource use? How serious are the errors of calculation and the slippages of control which we have described? What special virtues does it possess to set against these? The general tone of the discussion has probably left too strong an impression of waste and irrationality since the emphasis has been on problems. Waste and inefficiency certainly exist, but any real economy, and not least our own American economy, displays serious misallocations of resources. Even if the Soviet economy is considerably less than perfect, that is not a damning indictment. Actually, as will be seen when Soviet growth is discussed in the next chapter, the system has worked tolerably well in meeting the goals of growth and transformation of the economy which the leaders have set for it. But rather than trying to evaluate the performance of Soviet planning by a single criterion (we have seen what difficulties that gets Soviet controllers into!), it will be more to the point to conclude this chapter with an assessment of its distinctive strengths and weaknesses as a system for making decisions about resource use.

The Soviet structure is well designed for the attainment of a limited number of relatively well-defined goals. To the extent that the leaders can define their goals and priorities in a simple way, this system offers an effective way of mobilizing resources and effort to attain them. With its hierarchical structure and physical allocation of resources, it can effectively mobilize resources and control their gross allocation among end uses, programs, regions, and industries. So long as responsibility can be clearly defined for lower levels and so long as criteria for choice can be specified in a simple way, the commands will be fulfilled. The weaknesses that have been noted arise when these conditions are not met. As the range of choice increases for any decision maker, it becomes more difficult to make sure that commands will really control his behavior in conformance with central priorities. The more interdependence there is among economic decisions, the more difficult it becomes to give decision makers the kind of information and rules for choice that will guide them to rational decisions. The consequences of the propensity of the leaders to extend their values and prejudices beyond issues of ends to questions of means depend on the complexity of the means question. Stalin's equation of the growth of steel with growth in general was not a serious impropriety until technological development made available numerous other materials that could profitably be used in place of steel. The three cases discussed in the present chapter suggest that the effectiveness of the administrative approach depends on how many units are involved and how great the differentiation among them is. Such conditions require more detail and differentiation in plans directed to different units and more ability to make allowances for differences in performance among units than the information system can handle.

In short, any evaluation of the effectiveness of Soviet-style planning as a method of making decisions about resource use should be made in relation to the degree of complexity of the economy, its modernity, the degree of technological maturity and affluence that it has attained. In some areas the administrative approach works so badly that, despite their strong prejudice in favor of it, the Russians have sacrificed it to the market approach.

It seems fairly clear that, with growth, the weaknesses of the Soviet system have come to be more serious and its strengths less decisive. There is considerable evidence, both in their recent performance and in their own analyses, that the Russians' traditional forms of planning as we have described them are now becoming obsolete. The rate of growth has slowed, waste and inefficiency have become ever more apparent, and the responsiveness of the system to the wishes of its masters has been weakened. The analysis and conclusions of Soviet economists and planners who have tried to reason out the causes have much in common with what we have just propounded. Out of this situation there has grown a strong interest on the part of the leadership in "reforms of planning and administration" and some actual institutional changes aimed at decentralization (mentioned earlier in Chapter 3).

The basic principle of these reforms is to let an enterprise make more decisions on its own. In the reforms introduced in the consumer goods industries, for instance, an enterprise determines its own output plan by negotiating directly with its customers and drawing up contracts with them. It is also supposed to have similar freedom in arranging the purchases of inputs it makes from other firms. In making these contracts, the management has limited authority to establish prices, and failures to fulfill contracts are penalized by a system of strong financial sanctions. The director has more authority than in the past over personnel matters — such as the size of the labor force and differentiation of pay within the plant to motivate employees to concentrate on what is most important. Bonuses for managerial officials in the enterprise are made dependent on the amount of profit earned, rather than on the degree of fulfillment of numerous individual targets such as volume of output, the cost budget, and others. Many of these features were extended to all industry in modified form in 1965.

Important as these changes are, they fall far short of effecting real decentralization. They amount to a widening of the enterprises' rights in the sphere of *khozraschet* decision making described above but they have limited implications for the other spheres. For example, the nominal authority of the director to determine his own input and output mix is severely limited by the fact that he is still operating in an environment where, by and large, materials are still allocated by the material balancing process. Most important, the price system is still basically an administered system with prices set by bureaucrats rather than by supply and demand. This means, for example, that a buyer in any market, say, a machinery manufacturer who wants components of longer life and greater reliability, is still not free to use price bids to make the provision of such components profitable to the producer. In approving the reforms of 1965, the Central Committee did emphasize the importance of a price reform as an essential ingredient of the change but left the issue of price reform unresolved. A long-postponed price reform, most recently scheduled for the end of 1966, was dropped and a general overhaul of the price system was not expected before 1967. The problem is that the price setters have never been able to come to any agreement as to what constitute rational principles of pricing. Notwithstanding the presence today of a new elite who have a sophisticated understanding of the role that price should play in a decentralized system, the need to make price an item of negotiations in the lateral communication system is a point that most Soviet planners simply do not understand. All these difficulties have been demonstrated in the short experience with enterprises shifted to this kind of control. But perhaps the most interesting part of this experience is how difficult these enterprises found it to escape the traditional controls. When they tried to spend their profits as the new freedom supposedly allowed, bank officials would not permit it. The legal bodies which were supposed to enforce the new sanctions for contract violations applied the old ones instead. The established planning authorities continued to send them orders and interfere in their operations just as before. In other words, one feature of the environment in which these reforms are taking place is a large bureaucracy with a vested interest in doing things the old way and this may turn out to be a very serious obstacle to making the reforms effective. One of the important issues is, thus, whether the leaders in the reforms of 1965 have gone far enough in giving the new methods a chance to flourish and this is a question to which we will return in the final chapter.

6

Soviet Economic Growth

The question in this chapter and in the following one is — How good a job does the Soviet economy do? How well has it performed in achieving the various objectives that one might postulate for any economic system? How well has it done in fulfilling the special goals which the Soviet leadership has posed for it? The American public has been presented with a great variety of contradictory evidence on this score. Soviet achievements in space and in rapid growth are cited as evidence that the Soviet economy is ahead of, or in some way more effective than, ours. The low standard of living of the Soviet citizen and spectacular failures in some areas, such as agriculture, are alleged to prove the opposite. Such measures of economic performance are bound to be contradictory since each of them is only a partial measure. Obviously more general measures of performance are needed, some overall criteria of economic effectiveness in which all of these individual bits of evidence will be appropriately reflected. The first job is to elaborate such criteria.

Economists look at economic performance from two points of view, i.e., static and dynamic. The static aspect of performance concerns the effectiveness with which given resources are being used at a given point in time. The basic problem of any economic system is to use available labor, capital, and natural resources to obtain maximum possible output or, in a more general phrase, to maximize welfare. In previous chapters we have described the institutions and processes for handling this problem in the Soviet economy. But we also want to try to measure results, to judge how effectively resources have been employed.

The dynamic aspect of economic performance is concerned with growth and development, with improvements in productivity over time. Characteristically, as time passes, any economic system becomes more productive because of capital accumulation, improved utilization of resources, the discovery of new resources, and progress in the techniques of production. Again there is great heterogeneity in the performance of different economies in these respects and interpretation of these variations is an important problem. The present chapter discusses Soviet growth and the following chapter takes up the question of efficiency in the utilization of resources at a given time.

In the area of growth, Soviet economic performance has been impressive. At the end of forty years the leaders of the Soviet Union must be well satisfied with what has been accomplished. Soviet output has grown at rates not often equalled in world experience. This may seem a strange thing to say about a country where the average urban family lives in one small room and where black bread is still the staple of the average man's diet. But students of the Soviet economy generally agree that it is true. Our task here is to discuss the evidence and to explain how such rapid growth has been attained.

The Measurement of Output and Growth

In order to discuss the evidence intelligently, it is necessary first to explain some concepts used in measuring economic growth. Thinking about economic growth requires that one master a primer of four basic economic concepts. These are: (1) the notion of the gross national product (usually abbreviated as GNP) and its components, (2) the rate of growth of these magnitudes, (3) the notion of an index, and (4) the distinction between net and gross in relation to economic magnitudes.

The general idea of the gross national product can be described simply enough as the total output of a country's economy. The practice of national income accounting embraces a whole family of related concepts, differing in their precise definitions, but all intended to measure the total output of an economy during a given period such as a year. Thus when the United States Department of Commerce reports that the GNP of the United States in 1964 was 625 billion dollars, this means that the total amount of automobiles, new highways, clothing, and all the diverse outputs produced in that year was 625 billion dollars' worth. This total included not only the concrete physical objects produced for our use but also the value of such intangible "goods" as the services of doctors, teachers, television comedians, and many others.

For many purposes it is useful to know not only the total amount of output but also something about its composition. The total GNP can be broken down in various ways, of which two are important for our purposes here. (1) The first is according to end use — that is, how much of the total went for current satisfaction of people's wants, how much was invested in the creation of capital assets such as machines and factories, how much was used by the government for military and other purposes, and so on. (2) The second breakdown is according to the sector of origin. That is, how much of the total consisted of goods manufactured in factories, how much of agricultural output, how much of services. Both these classifications can be given in various degrees of fineness.

The absolute size of GNP tells little about economic performance or about efficiency. The GNP of India is much larger than that of Switzerland but this is because India is a much larger country than Switzerland, with more resources to draw on — not because it uses its resources more effectively than Switzerland. Indeed, the opposite is true. But to look at what happens to a nation's GNP as time passes gives us a useful measure of its economic performance and indeed the growth of GNP is one of the most commonplace measures of the progress of an economy. As time goes on, producers introduce better processes and more productive machinery, better organizational forms of production are adopted, the population acquires higher levels of education and skill, wasteful practices are increasingly eliminated, stocks of capital are accumulated. The supermarket replaces the corner grocery, steam locomotives are supplanted by the more efficient diesels, the horse gives way to the tractor, high-yield hybrid corn is invented, and so on, in a never-ending succession. These changes make possible a larger and larger output of goods and services, a bigger GNP, from a given amount of human effort.

Comparisons of economic magnitudes such as GNP or industrial output are often expressed by means of *indexes*. A series of figures on GNP, expressed in terms of dollars and shown in Table 6.1,

TABLE 6.1. United States GNP,
Measured in 1963 Prices

Year	In Billion Dollars	An an Index
1929	214.2	100
1933	150.5	70
1939	223.2	104
1944	391.1	183
1947	331.3	155
1950	374.0	175
1960	521.3	243
1963	585.0	273

can be translated into an index in the following way: A value of 100 is assigned to the figure for one of the years, called the base year, and then all the other figures in the series are assigned values on this scale indicating their size relative to the base year figure. For instance, if GNP in 1929 is taken as 100, then the index for GNP in 1963 would be 273 (i.e., 585.0 divided by 214.2 times 100) and so on for the other years. An index of 125 means an increase of 25 per cent over the base year and an index of 70 means a decline of 30 per cent from the level of the base year. Use of indexes also makes it possible to express diverse time series, such as GNP measured in dollars, employment measured in man-hours, Soviet GNP in rubles, or any other, all in terms of the same units.

How fast an economy grows is usually expressed in terms of the *percentage rate of growth* of GNP, industrial production, or other aggregates. The total output of the American economy in 1963 was 585 billion dollars, as against 563.6 billion dollars the year before, for an increase between 1962 and 1963 of 3.8 per

cent. (The index would be 103.8.) When we consider a longer
period of time, say, from 1950 to 1963, we speak of the *average
annual rate of growth,* also in per cent. Gross national product in
1950 was 374.0 billion dollars and in 1963 585.0 billion dollars.
On the average, if one starts with an output of 374 billion dollars
in 1950, by what percentage would output have to be raised each
successive year in order to end up with 585 billion dollars by
1963? The answer is 3.5 per cent per year.[1] Output did not actually
rise by just that percentage each year but, taking the period as a
whole, this was the average percentage growth from year to year.

On the whole that period was a good one for the economy of
the United States — mostly one of continued growth, interrupted
only by small and short-lived recessions. But our economy has
not always performed as well and in one not so distant period,
the decade of the Great Depression from 1929 to 1939, output
virtually stagnated. In other years it has grown faster. Taking the
whole period for which good statistics are available (i.e., since
1929) the average annual rate of growth has been about 3.0 per
cent. This is a fairly high rate of growth measured against the
long-term experience of other capitalist countries of the world,
though it has been surpassed on occasion.

For many economic magnitudes it is important to distinguish
gross and net measures. Consider, for instance, the notion of industrial output. How would one go about obtaining a figure for
the total output of industry in some country? He might add together the value of all industrial goods produced in a given year
or, what amounts to the same thing, add up the value of output of
all industrial enterprises. Such a measure would be called "gross
industrial output." It is called "gross" because there is much
double-counting in the result. This figure does not really tell how
many dollars' worth of goods industry has created in the given year
because the output of some industrial firms is consumed by other

---

[1] The formula for this and similar calculations is very simple, i.e.,
$374(x)^{13} = 585$. It simply recapitulates in the form of an equation the
question we asked above; namely, what number as applied to the preceding
year's output for 13 successive years will get us from an output of 374 billion dollars to one of 585 billion? The solution of the equation, $x = 1.035$,
means that the multiplier would have to be 1.035 which means an increase
of 3.5 per cent in each successive multiplication. So the average annual
rate of growth is 3.5 per cent.

industrial firms in producing their output. Thus the value of an automobile includes not only the value produced by the automobile factory but also the value of the steel that went into the automobile. So if the value of output of the steel mill and the value of output of the automobile plant are added together, the value of the steel is being counted twice in the total for all industrial output. Double-counting can be avoided by deducting from the value of goods produced by each industrial firm the value of the goods it has used up in turning out its product. Eliminating this double-counting gives what is called the "net output of industry."

Given this background of concepts, we are now ready to discuss in more careful detail the record of Soviet economic growth. The Russians claim that their economy has grown much faster than ours. They claim further that this differential in rates of growth is inevitable and that as a result sooner or later they will overtake and then surpass the capitalist part of the world in terms of economic power. As explained above, it is now generally agreed among economists working on these problems that the Soviet economy has grown faster than ours, even when the Soviet claims are discounted considerably. Whether or not they can overtake us and, if they can, how long it is likely to take obviously depends on whether this differential will continue in the future and, if it does, how large it will be. Predictions about the future are bound to be somewhat speculative but obviously one prerequisite for any such speculations about future growth is some solid information on what the rate of growth has been until now.

How fast Soviet national income and its components have grown turns out to be a very difficult question to deal with. An answer is made difficult by (1) the mendacity of Soviet statistics and the peculiarities of Soviet economic concepts and (2) by certain difficulties inherent in trying to measure the growth of aggregative economic magnitudes. Because the question of the Soviet rate of growth is a controversial one, concerning which there are widely divergent opinions current among the general public and some dispute even among the economists working on the problem, it is desirable to explain the essence of the problem as carefully as possible. Let us deal in turn with the two difficulties mentioned above.

The Deficiencies of Official Soviet Statistics on Growth

The official statistics computed and published by the Soviet government claim that in the period from 1928 to the present the average annual rate of growth of Soviet national income has been 9.5 per cent per year. (The Soviet concept of national income is not quite the same as our GNP, though both would probably grow at more or less the same rate.) This is so much above what other countries have achieved in comparable stages of industrialization that it appears on the face of it fantastic, impossible. Remember that the figure for the United States for the same period was 3.0 per cent per year. Knowing that Soviet statisticians have proclaimed that "statistics are a weapon in the class war," Western economists have suspected that these figures were somehow falsified or biased. And careful investigation of the methods used by the Russians in computing them does indeed show definite reasons for believing that they falsify the actual achievement. This is not to say that the Soviet statistics are simply made up out of thin air. Soviet planners and economists must have accurate statistics for their own planning and administrative work and it is the opinion of most Western economists that they do not keep two sets of figures — one for their own use and one to be published for the confusion of foreigners. Indeed, this would really be almost an impossibility. In a set of statistical data for a given economy there are many cross-checks, many tests for internal consistency. By and large our experience has been that the mass of Soviet statistics are more or less internally consistent and this reinforces the doubt that the Russians are engaged in a process of double bookkeeping or outright statistical falsification.

But a concept such as the gross national product, and even more its rate of growth, is an extremely complicated notion and an actual number purporting to measure it is derived only as the result of a complicated set of decisions about concept, definitions, rules for aggregation, and a long process of data manipulation. Choosing one set of rules or concepts rather than another may make a big difference in the final result of the calculation. After careful examination of Soviet practice in computing the GNP and its various components and in measuring its rate of growth, Western economists have concluded that the Russians have followed a set of rules and definitions which give an upward bias to the result. It is worth emphasizing here that the problem is not that all Soviet statistics are lies but that, in taking the raw data for their economy and processing it into an estimate of GNP, the Soviet statisticians follow procedures which exaggerate the rate of growth. So what Western economists have tried to do is to start over again with some of the original data and estimate independently their own indexes for the growth of GNP, industrial production, and other magnitudes. In doing this, their aim is to use rules and procedures that will make these indexes more nearly comparable in meaning to indexes compiled for the U.S. economy.

There is a large literature on the treacheries of Soviet statistics — too large to be effectively summarized here. But some of the difficulties of assessing Soviet economic growth can be illustrated by examination of one concrete example, namely, the measurement of the growth of Soviet industrial output. Industrial output is one of the major and at the same time the most rapidly growing component of Soviet gross national product. So it is precisely in this component that the biases will be most influential. The problems discussed here have parallels, though not always exact analogues, in measuring other components of GNP.

How Fast Has Soviet Industry Grown?

The Russians claim that industrial output was forty-four times larger in 1963 than it was in 1928 on the eve of the period of forced industrialization. But no one outside the Soviet Union takes this claim seriously. There are three main deficiencies in the way the Soviet statisticians compute their industrial output index — which make it a very inaccurate measure.

1. The Soviet claim refers to *gross industrial output*. In any year total output of industry is figured by first determining the value of output of every industrial enterprise and then adding these together. These annual totals are then compared with each other to get the index. Such a procedure involves much double-counting, as indicated above.

In GNP calculations, of course, this double-counting must be eliminated. What we are concerned with here, however, is not the absolute size of the real output of industry in a given year but rather its size relative to output in some other year. And the use of gross output to measure growth of industrial output will not *necessarily* introduce an error. If the percentage of industrial output consumed within industry does not change from year to year, then the index and rate of growth for gross industrial production will be identical with those for net industrial output.

But it is possible for the ratio of gross output to net output to change over time. One way this can happen is through organizational changes. Imagine, for instance, a large machinery factory which combines many successive processes in the manufacture of machinery. Pig iron may be turned into castings in its foundry; the castings may then be passed on to a machining shop where they are finished, and then on to an assembly shop where they are assembled into the final product. The factory may even have its own power plant which provides the electric power for the other parts of the plant. The output of this machinery plant would be measured by the total value of goods it finished and sold to other enterprises in the economy.

Imagine that now, without changing any of the processes or the number of workers or the amount of output, the plant is split into four separate units — a foundry, a machining shop, an electric plant, and the assembly plant. The whole complex works just as before and the only difference is that since each of the former shops is now an independent enterprise, each sells its output to the other parts of the plant. What is the output of this collection of plants now? If one follows the Soviet procedure of determining the value of output of each enterprise and adds these together, the total output will obviously be much larger than before. The output of the assembly plant remains the same as the entire complex before it was split up but now added to it is the output of the three newly separated enterprises.

Has output really increased? Obviously not, but if one simply looks at the figures on gross output, computed by the same rule each year, it appears that there has been a large increase in output. Such changes can also take place in the opposite direction, when formerly independent enterprises are merged or when there is a decrease in specialization. But most observers think that the trend has been mostly the other way in the Soviet economy. There are two good reasons for this. Along with the growth of the scale of output almost always comes specialization, leading to a larger number of stages in the processing. Also there is a great institutional bias favoring splits and opposing mergers in the Soviet economy. In the Soviet system of planned economy the main criterion by which officials at all levels of administration of industry are judged is whether or not they are increasing the output of the plants under their jurisdiction as measured by the gross output concept. Imagine that you are the minister of some important industry. You would not be at all displeased to get an easy gain in output as in the illustration above but you would be greatly distressed to have to report the loss the figures would show if you recombined the plants. So you would use all your influence to prevent the merging of the plants. There is virtually no way of telling just how important this factor is as a bias in the index of Soviet industrial output but most economists think that some of the growth in the Soviet index of output has come about by this process.

2. Another influence which exaggerates the Soviet measure of industrial growth has been failure to correct adequately for changes in the price level. Since the object of an industrial output index is to measure the growth in the actual physical volume of production, it is necessary to take care to eliminate any distortion caused by changes in price. Imagine, for instance, that a tractor plant puts out 5,000 tractors in a given year and that the price per tractor is 10,000 rubles. The total output of the plant would then be 50 million rubles. If in the next year it again produces 5,000 tractors and the price has risen to 12,000 rubles, the value of its output that year would be 60 million rubles. But clearly there has been no increase in real output; the rise from 50 million to 60 million rubles reflects only the price change. Obviously to measure output in terms of rubles, it is necessary to use the same prices in both years. By and large the Soviet statisticians have tried to use "constant" prices. In reporting the value of its output every year for inclusion in the all-industry total, the Soviet enterprise has been instructed to figure out the value of its output in "constant prices." Until 1950 the prices that existed in 1926–27 were used as "constant prices." So far so good. But in an economy such as that of the Soviet Union, which was being transformed from a backward to a modern one at a very fast rate, there inevitably arose many situations when a 1926–27 price was required for a com-

pletely new product, one that had not been produced anywhere in the Soviet Union in 1926–27. Given the pressure to report growth, enterprise directors often valued these new products at artificially high "1926–27 prices." The rapid inflation made the high prices seem more credible. Of course, even at higher levels of administration there was some disinclination to quarrel with such exaggerations on the part of plant management because people at the higher levels also liked to be able to report large increases in output to their superiors. One cannot very well imagine the head of the Central Statistical Administration, for instance, telling Stalin that the index of industrial output they were passing on to him was actually higher than reality warranted.

The 1926–27 prices have now been abandoned and the prices of a more recent year are now used as constant prices in figuring the changing volume of output. But it is still possible to perform certain kinds of manipulations, and Soviet industrial managers have become very adept at feeling out such loopholes in the system of control. Under pressure to increase the output of his plant, are there any ways a plant manager can make the same amount of output look bigger on paper? One thing he might do is redesign some of his products slightly so that they can be labeled as new products. For these new products, of course, there are no constant prices since they were not being produced in the year from which constant prices are taken. The present rules say that the constant price for such new products is the temporary price set for them in the first period of their production. So the plant manager has his bookkeeping department or planning department draw up cost calculations showing excessively high cost estimates and on this basis tries to persuade the price-setting authorities to set a high price for the new machine. As a result, he can turn out the same number of machines as last year, machines which are essentially identical with last year's machines and require about the same amount of labor and raw materials to produce, but which have a higher value in "constant" prices than the old machines.

Just how important a bias this has been in the Soviet index no one knows. It is thought to be fairly important in the machinery and chemical industries, for example, where there is a constant introduction of new products.

3. The third quarrel with the Soviet index of industrial production is the weighting system on which it is based. The use of

1926–27 prices raises the Soviet index above what it would be if the prices of some other year had been used. This weighting bias is a rather complex phenomenon but it is not particularly difficult to understand if we explain it on the basis of a simplified example. In the process we will have to add something to what has already been said about index numbers.

Imagine a hypothetical economy with a very simple industry sector, producing only two industrial products, tractors and shoes. Assume that data on the output and prices of these products in two different years are as given in Table 6.2. The question to be answered is — "What is the index of industrial output in the second year, compared to the first?" Or to put it in another way — How much has total industrial output grown between the two years?

Clearly it is improper just to compare the rubles' worth of output in the two years since much of the increase from 2.5 million rubles to 24 million rubles has been caused by the rise in prices rather than by a real growth in physical output. To make a valid comparison, it is necessary to value the output of both years in identical prices. One possible approach would be to calculate what the value of output in 1939 *would have been if prices had not risen since 1926* and then compare this with the actual value of output in 1926 which of course is already measured in 1926 prices. This is done in Table 6.3. Total output in 1939, measured in 1926 prices, is 7 million rubles (MR) as compared to 2.5 MR in 1926. If these figures are converted to index form, the index of output in 1939 would be 280.

This index number just computed will acquire some additional meaning if it is explained that it can be determined via a somewhat different computational route, as follows: If the output of shoes and tractors are considered separately, an index of output can be determined for each without using any prices at all, just by comparing the physical amounts in the two years. Thus in 1939 the index for tractors is 400 and for shoes, 100. The index for all industry is obviously somewhere in between these two, some sort of an average of them. But if one examines the situation in 1926, it appears that tractors made up more than half of total industrial output, shoes less than half. Since the two commodities are not of equal importance, we do not want a simple average of the two indexes in which we would just add them and divide by two. Instead we want an average which combines the separate commodity

TABLE 6.2. Data for the Computation
of an Industrial Output Index

	1926 Output	1926 Prices	Value in 1926 Prices	1939 Output	1939 Prices	Value in 1939 Prices
Tractors	500	3,000 R	1.5 MR	2,000	9,000 R	18 MR
Shoes	20,000	50 R	1 MR	20,000	300 R	6 MR
Total	—	—	2.5 MR	—	—	24 MR

TABLE 6.3. Computation of Industrial Output
Index Using 1926 Prices

	1926 Output	1926 Prices	Value in 1926 Prices	1939 Output	1926 Prices	Value in 1926 Prices
Tractors	500	3,000 R	1.5 MR	2,000	3,000 R	6 MR
Shoes	20,000 prs.	50 R	1 MR	20,000 prs.	50 R	1 MR
Total	—	—	2.5 MR	—	—	7 MR
Index			100			280

TABLE 6.4. Computation of Industrial Output
Index Using 1939 Prices

	1926 Output	1939 Prices	Value in 1939 Prices	1939 Output	1939 Prices	Value in 1939 Prices
Tractors	500	9,000 R	4.5 MR	2,000	9,000 R	18 MR
Shoes	20,000 prs.	300 R	6 MR	20,000 prs.	300 R	6 MR
Total	—	—	10.5 MR	—	—	24 MR
Index			100			229

indexes in the proper proportions, which gives the separate indexes their proper weight in the average index. Such an index is called a "weighted" index. Since tractors make up 60 per cent of total output and shoes 40 per cent, we make up the weighted average by adding together 60 per cent of the tractor index and 40 per cent of the shoe index as below.

$$\underset{\text{index}}{\text{Tractor}} \times \underset{\substack{\text{cent of} \\ \text{total output}}}{\text{Tractors as per}} + \underset{\text{index}}{\text{Shoe}} \times \underset{\substack{\text{cent of} \\ \text{total output}}}{\text{Shoes as per}} = \underset{\text{index}}{\text{Weighted}}$$

$$400 \times .60 + 100 \times .40 = 240 + 40 = 280$$

←NOTE TO TABLES: The formula for the weighted index, starting from the information on outputs and prices given to Table 6.2 can be spelled out as follows where T stands for tractors and S for shoes.

$$\frac{\dfrac{1939\ \text{output of T}}{1926\ \text{output of T}} \times \begin{matrix}1926\ \text{price}\\ \text{of T}\end{matrix} \times \begin{matrix}1926\ \text{output of T}\end{matrix} \quad + \quad \dfrac{1939\ \text{output of S}}{1926\ \text{output of S}} \times \begin{matrix}1926\ \text{price}\\ \text{of S}\end{matrix} \times \begin{matrix}1926\ \text{output of S}\end{matrix}}{\begin{matrix}1926\\ \text{output}\\ \text{of T}\end{matrix} \times \begin{matrix}1926\\ \text{price}\\ \text{of T}\end{matrix} + \begin{matrix}1926\\ \text{output}\\ \text{of S}\end{matrix} \times \begin{matrix}1926\\ \text{price}\\ \text{of S}\end{matrix} \quad \begin{matrix}1926\\ \text{output}\\ \text{of T}\end{matrix} \times \begin{matrix}1926\\ \text{price}\\ \text{of T}\end{matrix} + \begin{matrix}1926\\ \text{output}\\ \text{of S}\end{matrix} \times \begin{matrix}1926\\ \text{price}\\ \text{of S}\end{matrix}}$$

The reader can easily satisfy himself that this expression reduces to

$$\begin{matrix}\text{Index of output}\\ \text{of T}\end{matrix} \times \begin{matrix}\text{T as per cent}\\ \text{of total out-}\\ \text{put in 1926}\end{matrix} + \begin{matrix}\text{Index of output}\\ \text{of S}\end{matrix} \times \begin{matrix}\text{S as per cent}\\ \text{of total out-}\\ \text{put in 1926}\end{matrix}$$

Looking back at the longer formula, the numerator can be simplified by cancelling out the terms denoting output in 1926. When this is done, the formula becomes

$$\frac{\begin{matrix}1939\ \text{output of T}\end{matrix} \times \begin{matrix}1926\ \text{price of T}\end{matrix} + \begin{matrix}1939\ \text{output of S}\end{matrix} \times \begin{matrix}1926\ \text{price of S}\end{matrix}}{\begin{matrix}1926\ \text{output of T}\end{matrix} \times \begin{matrix}1926\ \text{price of T}\end{matrix} + \begin{matrix}1926\ \text{output of S}\end{matrix} \times \begin{matrix}1926\ \text{price of S}\end{matrix}}$$

which is identical with the computation carried out in Table 6.3. Thus a procedure in which we weight indexes for individual commodities is formally identical with one in which we compute value of output in constant prices. We can use or think in terms of whichever one is more convenient.

This approach gives the same index as before, i.e. 280, because arithmetically it actually amounts to the same computation as was performed in Table 6.3.

In the discussion so far, 1926 prices have been used as the constant prices for comparing total output in the two years but we could just as well use 1939 prices. That is, we could figure the total industrial output in each year, valued in 1939 prices, and then compare these values to get an index of output. This approach is carried out in Table 6.4 and it turns out that total output of industry rose from 10.5 MR in 1926 to 24 MR in 1939 which gives an index of 229. But the index figured earlier, in which 1926 prices were used, was 280. Why is the answer different when 1939 prices are used as the constant prices?

Essentially the answer is that the prices of tractors and shoes relative to each other were different in 1939 from what they were in 1926. The influence of this change in relative prices can be most easily comprehended by thinking in terms of the weighted index approach to getting the overall index. It will be remembered that using the 1926 prices was equivalent to getting a weighted average for all industry by taking 60 per cent of the tractor index and 40 per cent of the shoe index. These percentages were the respective percentages of the two commodities in total output in 1926 valued in 1926 prices. But if the 1926 output is valued in 1939 prices, it turns out that tractors were only 43 per cent of total output rather than 60 per cent and shoes were 57 per cent rather than only 40 per cent. The relative share of tractors and shoes in total output in 1926 is different when figured in 1939 prices from what it is when figured in 1926 prices because tractors were less valuable relative to shoes in the 1939 price structure than in the 1926 price structure. If these percentages are inserted in the formula for the weighted index approach, the result is

$$\frac{\text{Tractor}}{\text{index}} \times 43 \text{ per cent} + \frac{\text{Shoe}}{\text{index}} \times 57 \text{ per cent}$$

$$400 \times .43 + 100 \times .57 = 229$$

Using 1939 prices gives more emphasis in our average to the growth of the shoe industry, which is low (in fact, no growth at all), and less to the growth of the tractor industry, which is quite high. The result, naturally, is a lower average index for industry as a whole.

Now precisely the kind of situation illustrated by the data of our example has been very common in the Soviet industrial sector. Those commodities which have grown the most have also experienced declines in their prices relative to other, slower-growing commodities. This is typical of the early industrialization experience of most countries. In such a period those outputs which grow fastest are generally the ones that experience the greatest increases in efficiency of production and therefore also experience reductions in costs and prices relative to other goods. As the Soviet Union industrialized, the output of "traditional" commodities like shoes did not increase much and no great gains were made in the productivity of the shoe industry. But the output of such producers goods as tractors increased very rapidly, and because these were new branches of production, there were great gains in the efficiency with which such products were produced and a lowering of their costs and prices relative to other goods. Thus the use of the prices of the year 1926–27, i.e., an early year, has given the Soviet statisticians an index with a markedly higher rate of growth than if they had used the prices of some later year as weights.

Eventually the Russians themselves decided that they could not continue planning and measuring output by an index computed in 1926–27 prices. From 1950 on, the index of industrial output has been computed using more recent prices — those of 1952 for the Fifth Five-Year Plan period and those of 1955 for 1956 and after. Hence the index for recent years is probably not appreciably biased by inappropriate price weights. But the index for earlier years is still based on the 1926–27 prices as weights so that the Soviet claims about growth for the whole period since the twenties must still be discounted.

The Index Number Problem ✗

Economists label the ambiguity presented by the two different indexes "the index number problem." It goes considerably beyond the specific problem of measuring industrial growth considered here and it bedevils many other aspects of our evaluation of Soviet economic performance as well. It affects measurement of GNP growth and also confuses the issue of the size of Soviet output compared with that of other countries. Since the index number problem is so important in evaluating Soviet economic performance, we must consider a bit more carefully just what is at stake in this ambiguity. Which of these two numbers is the best measure of the growth of Soviet industrial output?

An answer requires first that we specify more exactly what we are trying to measure. When the weighting alternatives are interpreted in economic terms, it becomes clear that they involve alternative assumptions about value, difficulties of production, or scarcity. The two indexes obtained in Tables 6.3 and 6.4 really answer two different questions. The index of 290 answers the question, "On the assumption tractors were as valuable relative to shoes in 1939 as they were in 1926, how much bigger would the total output in 1939 be than in 1926?" The lower index is an answer to the question, "Assuming that tractors were only as valuable relative to shoes in 1926 as they later became in 1939, how much has output grown?" Obviously, neither assumption fits the facts of the case. This suggests that the choice between weighting systems depends on what question the index is being asked to answer. What should be the meaning of a statement that output has doubled? One possibility would be to have it mean that the output of each and every commodity doubled, but since in real life the output of different commodities grows at different rates, such a conception would be too confining. Actually we want a statement that output has doubled to mean a doubling of something more abstract than actual output — i.e., capacity to produce goods in general (what the economist calls "production potential"). In the light of this definition of the growth concept, the index number problem exists because the relative burden which different goods put on production potential changes with industrialization. During growth, some goods become cheaper relative to others, so that an answer to the question of how much production potential has grown depends on specifying what kind of goods we want it to produce. Its capacity to produce an assortment in which goods with falling costs predominate increases faster than its capacity to produce an assortment with a higher proportion of relatively more costly goods. Without going into the complex details of the argument, we may simply assert that measurements using early year weights are likely to be a better measure of change in capacity to produce the late year mixes and vice-versa for measures using late year mixes. Subject to some reservations, our index of 290 tells the changing capacity to produce the 1939 mix of shoes and tractors, while the 229 measures the changing capacity to produce the 1926 proportions. Seen in this way, the index of 290 is probably preferable as a measure of growth. After all, one of the main objectives of the industrialization effort was to move from the mixes characteristic of a relatively unindustrialized country to a more modern and industrialized mix. Hence the changing capacity to produce late year mixes is the one relevant to an evaluation of growth.

Of course, the choice of a rate of growth will depend on what use one is going to make of it. Without being dogmatic about the matter, however, the implication of the above discussion seems to be that one should be suspicious of any attempt to downgrade Soviet growth which depends on emphasizing indexes using late year weights.

Western Computations of Soviet Growth

In their research on the Soviet economy, economists outside the Soviet Union have put much effort into deriving independent estimates of Soviet growth to replace the exaggerated claims made by the Russians. Some of this research has been concerned with the growth of the economy as a whole, i.e., with the growth of gross national product. Other more specialized studies have estimated the rate of growth for industrial output, for agriculture, other sectors of the economy, and for individual end uses such as investment, military spending, and consumption. The principal study of GNP growth is that conducted by Abram Bergson and his associates for the RAND Corporation. The following description of Soviet growth performance draws heavily on that research.

In the early stages of the Soviet development push, estimates of growth depend on the weighting system used. Evaluated in 1928 prices, the GNP growth between 1928 and 1937 was very high — 11.9 per cent per year. When 1937 prices are used, the rate turns out to have been about 5.5 per cent per year which is still quite a high rate of growth compared with other historical examples of industrialization. For the period since 1937 the choice of weights influences the outcome much less drastically. Between 1937 and 1958 output somewhat more than doubled, for an annual average rate of growth of about 4 per cent per year. This result, of course, reflects strongly the experience of the Second World War when, instead of growing, output declined. For the years since the Second World War the rate of growth is more nearly 6 per cent per year. (Remember that the comparable figure for the United States since 1947 has been about 3.5 per cent per year.) Any conclusions as to the rate of growth over the entire period since 1928 depends strongly on whether one takes the high or low rate for the years 1928–37. If that period is counted in in terms of the 1928 price basis, the result for the entire history of Soviet industrialization is an average annual growth rate for GNP of a little over 6 per cent per year. If the prices of later years are used throughout, the overall rate of growth is a little less than 5 per cent per year. Of these figures, the one most germane to the issue of the catching-up process is the figure of around 6 per cent in the period since World War II.

Within this overall picture of growth, there has been sharply differentiated growth among sectors and uses. The highest rates have been achieved in industry and construction. The result of several studies of industrial growth are compared in Table 6.5 with

TABLE 6.5. Indexes of Soviet Industrial Production*

	1928	1937	1940	1950	1955	1961
Official Soviet	100	445	583	1,009	1,866	3,333
(1950 = 100)				100	184	330
Hodgman	100	371	430	646	—	—
Jasny	100	287	330–350	411	—	—
Nutter	100	263	209	389	566	—
Kaplan-Moorsteen	100	249	263	369	583	—
Greenslade-Wallace	—	—	—	100	163	268

* The studies from which these indexes are taken are listed in the Suggestions for Further Reading at the end of the book.

the official Soviet claims. As can be seen, there are considerable differences among Western estimates, reflecting different method-ologies and different weighting systems. Nevertheless, all these re-calculations have found rates of growth within a range quite distinct from the officially claimed Soviet rate of growth. They suggest that output grew by 10–11 times between 1928 and 1961 (a little over 7 per cent per year) rather than by a factor of 33 times as the Russians claim. But an average rate of industrial growth of 7–8 per cent sustained over a period of 33 years is a very impressive record in the light of world experience of economic growth.

At the other extreme of the performance spectrum is agriculture. Farm output actually declined during the early years of the Soviet growth effort and two decades later, by 1950, had barely surpassed the level already achieved in 1928. After 1950, agriculture began to grow fairly rapidly in response to some radical changes in agri-cultural policy and the Russians claim that by 1963 gross output of agriculture was about two and a half times what it had been in 1928. Research by scholars outside the Soviet Union suggests that growth was actually somewhat less than this, with output perhaps having doubled.[2]

Considering that the population has grown by one-half in these years, it is easy to understand why the problem of agriculture remains a crucial one for the Soviet policy makers.

The transportation sector also experienced a high rate of growth but more so in freight traffic than in passenger traffic. In developing economies the transport job grows rapidly compared with other kinds of output, as the mix of productive activities shifts in the direction of more bulky commodities (such as fuels, heavy raw materials, lumber and construction materials) and as regional specialization proceeds.

A large part of the national income in modern economics originates in the production of various services — education and research, health care, wholesale and retail trade, housing, government administration, and others. Growth in this part of the economy has been heterogeneous. Some of these activities, such as research, education, and health care, are as important for the attainment of state objectives as for the fulfillment of consumer wants and objectives and have experienced rapid growth in the U.S.S.R. Others, catering more exclusively to consumer goals, such as housing, utilities, and municipal services, have grown relatively slowly.

Looked at by end use, the fastest growing parts of the Soviet economy have been the military program, investment, and such state-provided services as health and education. The use of resources for military purposes has grown faster than any other major use — i.e., about 12–15 per cent per year over the whole period. In 1937 prices, investment grew at almost 8 per cent per year, compared with the average GNP growth of a little less than 5 per cent. Consumption, on the other hand, actually declined in the early years of industrialization and subsequently rose only slowly. As late as 1950, per capita consumption had advanced little, if at all, beyond the level which Soviet citizens had enjoyed in 1928. Thus up until about 1950 the Soviet regime employed the incre-

---

[2] Measurement of agricultural growth is much complicated by changes in the territory of the U.S.S.R. The Soviet Union has had an appreciably larger territory since 1939 than it had in 1928. The statements above refer to agricultural output on the respective territory at each end of the period.

ments of output made available by growth almost exclusively for state ends and did not permit the population to share to any appreciable degree in the results of growth. Apart from allocating enough of the additional output to provide the traditional ration of consumption goods and services to the added population, it employed all the gains from economic development for such state goals as investment and military strength. Since 1950, however, the consumer has been treated somewhat more generously. There have been important variations from year to year but, taking the period since 1950 as a whole, the consumption share of GNP has grown pari passu with other uses. This means that it has also grown much faster than the Soviet population, with the result that per capita consumption has increased considerably. This improvement has been fast enough to impress Soviet citizens and to inspire both a certain loyalty to the regime and great expectations for the future.

Factors Underlying Growth

The Soviet growth achievement can be explained in various ways and at various levels of concreteness. A great deal has been said already about the general background circumstances — the Soviet leaders have made growth a high priority objective and have honored this priority both in the kind of administrative structure they have devised for running the economy and in the allocational choices they have made. But in the context of this chapter, it is interesting to relate the growth of output to a more specific cause, i.e., the growth in the flow of inputs. One explanation for the growth of any economy is that with the passage of time the amount of resources devoted to production, especially the supplies of capital and labor, increases and it appears that much of Soviet growth can be explained in this way.

The favoring of investment in Soviet allocational priorities meant a rapid increase in capital stock. The Russians claim that their stock of fixed capital has grown by about 10 times, i.e., faster than output and much faster than any of the other important inputs. One form of capital not caught in this measure is investment in human resources — the regime has invested heavily in upgrading the general skills of the population. If one compares the amount of investment embodied in the present population (i.e., in terms of

how much resources have gone into their education and training)
with the situation three and a half decades ago, there turns out to
be a tremendous growth in this input also. Labor input has grown
considerably and it is significant that it has grown faster than the
population. This was made possible by favorable changes in the
age structure of the population which increased the share of the
population in the main working ages and by favorable changes in
participation rates (i.e., the percentage of people of working ages
who actually work), especially on the part of women. Also, the
average number of hours worked per person probably increased
somewhat. This disparity in expansion of the capital stock and the
labor force was no doubt a highly favorable circumstance for
growth. It meant that rather than scrambling to keep new entrants
into the labor force supplied with the same amount of capital as
existing workers had, it was possible to raise the ratio of capital to
labor and to embody more modern technology in the newly created
production facilities.

The expansion of the labor force relative to the population also
raises another interesting question. One of the remarkable features
of Soviet development is that the Soviet population has grown quite
slowly — i.e., at a rate somewhat over one-half of one per cent
per year. This was no doubt a good thing — the Soviet Union
somehow escaped the problem of a "population explosion" that is
so frequently an obstacle to economic development. Economically
underdeveloped countries usually have high birth rates balanced
by high death rates and thus relatively slow population growth.
Efforts to stimulate economic development usually upset this balance — they are likely to mean big reductions in death rates quite
early (especially in infant mortality) as a result of better nutrition
and public health. But reductions in *birth rates* do not follow at
once, with the result that population growth accelerates. This frus-
trates efforts to raise per capita income and the per capita endowment of capital needed to increase productivity. That the Russians
escaped this problem seems to owe little to planning or conscious
policy. The natural fertility of the Soviet population seems to have
remained high and the death rate under natural conditions did
drop remarkably, as did also infant mortality. But population
growth was averted by successive catastrophes which killed off
millions of people and which limited the reproductive potential of

the population by upsetting the sex ratio. Emigration, civil war, famines, deportations to labor camps, and the Second World War resulted in the loss of millions of lives and prevented the birth of millions who would have been born if conditions had been normal. On balance, these population disasters probably made growth easier. It is difficult to believe that the Russians would have been able to do what they did in the way of investment and modernization if they had had to cope in the process with feeding, clothing, and housing the additional millions of persons that normal population dynamics would have given them. But the fact remains that these consequences were unintended and thoroughly deplorable from any humanistic point of view. Soviet central planning *per se* has not disclosed any acceptable answer to the problem of population growth and this is one aspect of the Soviet growth experience which underdeveloped countries would not want to emulate.

When we consider all inputs together, their supply has not grown as rapidly as output, leaving a considerable part of growth to be accounted for by changes in productivity. One would expect the Russians to have made extraordinary gains in productivity. They were in a position to borrow technological improvements from more advanced countries without themselves having to make large investments in research and development and in the early forms of technology that are made obsolete by later developments. They could overleap the long process of experimentation that characterizes the development of any big innovation. This kind of technological borrowing is an advantage which any underdeveloped country has, and the Russians resorted to it on a grand scale. They took as models the most advanced machinery designs, plant layout, and processes they could find in developed countries and created fairly modern industries by replicating these units over and over again. In the thirties, in particular, they imported large amounts of advanced equipment and employed foreign consultants to design and supervise the construction of new plants copied from the most advanced Western European or American designs. But the interesting thing is that, despite this advantage in being able to borrow technology, Soviet progress in productivity does not seem to have been exceptional. The rate of increase in resource productivity does not seem to differ much from that achieved in other countries. This obviously implies that exceptional growth should be attributed more to the ability of Soviet command planning to mobilize resources — i.e., to accumulate capital, to educate on a mass scale, to move people from low productivity occupations such as agriculture to high productivity ones such as industry, and to force increases in participation rates — than to any special ability to use resources efficiently and increase their productivity.

Recent Performance

The period of Soviet history which probably comes closest to what might be called "normalcy," and a fair test of the capabilities of the system, is the period following the Second World War. Altogether, the first dozen or so years in this period, say, up to about 1958, were years of successful, dynamic performance. They were bleak ones in terms of human values, and such traditional weaknesses of the Soviet economy as recurrent crises, waste, and emphasis on state ends at the expense of private ones were much in evidence. But growth continued apace, even in the problem sector of agriculture, and the Soviet populace was at last beginning to draw some benefits after two decades of sacrifice. That experience seemed to justify strongly an optimistic evaluation of the prospects for catching up with the more advanced capitalist countries. With the United States GNP growing at 3–3.5 per cent and the Soviet at 6–7 per cent per year, it looked as if the boast that it was only a matter of time until the Russians would surpass America in total output and output per capita was well founded. That vision has been tarnished in more recent years, however, by an unmistakable slowdown in the rate of expansion. In each year from 1958 to 1963 the percentage increase in Soviet GNP declined, compared with the previous year. This slowdown owed much to stagnation or decline in agricultural output but there was also a consistent deceleration in industrial growth. The exact extent of the decline remains controversial but from the 6–7 per cent annual GNP growth rates of most of the postwar period, the increase in output declined to as low as 2.5 per cent in 1963 according to one estimate. It would be misleading to stress unduly that particular estimate or that particular year — a disaster in agriculture that owed much to exceptionally bad weather is an important part of the explanation. But even when we look at a somewhat longer stretch of time, it does seem undeniable that there has been a serious decline in the dynamism of the Soviet economy since 1958. We will return to an interpretation of this deceleration and an evaluation of its meaning in the concluding chapter but at this point it is sufficient simply to report it as part of the overall growth record.

Our general conclusions about Soviet growth might be summarized in a few words as follows. Considering the whole history of its development effort, the Soviet Union has achieved under planning a remarkably high average rate of growth. It has been a highly variegated record, with much better performance in some sectors than in others. Impressive growth and modernization in some sectors have been combined with virtual stagnation in others. But these failures are partly the result of conscious choices rather than of inadequate planning. The leaders chose deliberately to assign consumption to a subordinate place in their hierarchy of values and as a consequence were willing to avoid any real effort to increase agricultural output. There has also been considerable variation in performance when shorter time periods are distinguished. In particular, the last few years have witnessed an appreciable deceleration of the rate of growth.

7

The Soviet Economy: Size, Allocation, and Productivity

The Soviet Union has done very well in the area of growth, but growth is only one aspect of economic performance and we are curious to know something about other measures as well. What is the size of the Russians' aggregate output? How is Soviet GNP allocated among major end uses? How productively does the Soviet system use the resources at its disposal? To answer these questions, we turn to look at a number of relationships and ratios referring to input and output within a given year rather than to trends over time.

Official Soviet statistics are not a reliable source to which one can refer routinely for current information on the gross national product of the Soviet Union. The Russians do compute measures of aggregate output but their definitions of these concepts are quite different from ours. Moreover, they publish very little concrete data from the calculations of national income and product as they make them. As a result, western analysts of the Soviet economy have had to compile their own estimates of Soviet income and product by manipulating more detailed information. Estimation of Soviet GNP in this way, even for one year, is a large undertaking and as a result the various estimates made outside the U.S.S.R. cover only selected years and cannot always be reconciled with each other. Since to be done well such a study must wait upon the appearance of sufficient data, the firmest estimates refer to periods several years past. Fortunately, the general picture of the size, distribution, and origin of Soviet GNP which emerges from the latest available studies is generally representative of more recent years as well.

Soviet GNP by End Use

Soviet GNP in 1958, classified by the various purposes to which it is put, is shown in Column (1) of Table 7.1.

This estimate was put together by gathering or estimating expenditures on each of the major uses to which the income of the society was directed. This means, of course, that each of these components of output is valued and added into the total at the prices at which it was bought and sold in the Soviet economy. In an economy of the Soviet type, the prices at which goods are transferred from seller to buyer are unfortunately often a poor measure of their real cost or value. Under the Soviet price system some goods are priced high enough to cover not only their production cost but also to provide a large income to the government in the form of taxes and profits. Other goods have virtually no taxes levied on them and indeed may be sold at prices below the actual cost of producing them. Whole industries in the Soviet economy have often operated at a considerable loss, while in other industries prices are set high enough to return large profits. Remember also that no charges are made in the Soviet price system for the services of capital or for the use of natural resources; the prices set for goods produced with the aid of these resources thus understate their true cost. What is more important, this omission is much greater for some goods and industries than others so that the *relative* cost of different goods is distorted.

A valid measure of how the Russians allocate their resources among various purposes, therefore, requires corrections for these peculiarities of the Soviet price system. One must remove from the value shown for consumption expenditure, for example, such elements as turnover taxes, which represent an arbitrary markup rather than a real resource cost, correct for any subsidies or losses, and include an appropriate interest charge for the capital used in producing consumption goods. The impact of these corrections will be quite differentiated between different categories so that the distribution of income by end use is changed appreciably. The last two columns in Table 7.1 represent this more accurate statement

TABLE 7.1. Soviet GNP by End Use, 1958

	(1)	(2)	(3)
	At market prices (BR)	In adjusted prices (BR)	Percent of total
Consumption	99.51	75.95	59.6
Goods	77.45	54.71	42.9
(of which, consumption in kind)	12.62	12.32	9.7
Health and Education	12.80	12.15	9.5
Other Services	9.26	9.09	7.1
Defense	9.06	8.68	6.8
Gross Investment	42.44	40.32	31.6
Public	40.98	38.93	30.5
Private	1.46	1.39	1.1
Government Administration	2.70	2.54	2.0
Total	153.71	127.49	100

Source: Nimitz, Nancy, *Soviet National Income and Product, 1956–1958,* Santa Monica, 1962.

of the allocation of GNP by end use. The effect of this adjustment has been to raise the share of investment and military programs and to reduce the share of consumption. Since the turnover tax falls primarily on household consumption, its share in total GNP is much smaller than in terms of the prices at which goods are actually sold.

Before we leave these figures, we should add that they probably understate the real share of military expenditures in Soviet GNP. They are based on the official statement about military expenditures given in the Soviet budget but there is good reason to believe that the Russians conceal significant amounts of military expenditure under other headings in their budget. Because the Russians are so careful to maintain secrecy about the magnitude of their resource allocations to military needs, there is very little to go on in adjusting this published figure for the supposed omissions. But the informed opinion of those who have worked on this question seems to be that a comprehensive figure for Soviet military expenditures would amount to 9–10 per cent of GNP. Adjusting the figures of Table 7.1 on this assumption and taking into account some slight shifts among other use categories that have taken place since 1958, the Soviet allocation pattern in the early sixties would compare with the U.S. pattern as shown below.

	Share in Total GNP (per cent)	
	U.S.	U.S.S.R.
Consumption	66.8	55.8
Defense	10.0	9.5
Investment	19.4	33.1
Government Administration	3.7	1.6

The most striking difference between the Soviet and American distributions is the very high share of investment and the low share of consumption in the Soviet economy. In the Soviet Union, investment has consistently accounted for over 25 per cent of GNP in postwar years and in many years it has been over 30 per cent. In the United States, investment has usually fallen within the range 18–20 per cent. The high rate of investment in the Soviet Union is all the more remarkable in view of the relatively smaller output of the Soviet economy and the many other demands on it. How much of its national income a society can afford to devote to investment depends partly on the level of national income. An analogy with an individual family can help us appreciate this relationship. The family with an income of $50,000 per year can live very well indeed and still have a considerable share of its income left over for saving and investment, but another family of the same size with an income of $3,000 can scarcely expect to save any of its income. The same principle applies to nations. In terms of per capita income, the Soviet Union is more nearly comparable with some relatively underdeveloped countries, in which the rate of investment is usually quite low, than it is to the United States. In the years since the Second World War a number of developed countries have devoted to investment nearly as high a share of GNP as the U.S.S.R. and in some cases an even higher share.

But in most of these countries the competing claim of military expenditures has been kept to a figure appreciably below the 10 per cent or so of GNP so used by the Russians.

The internal composition of Soviet investment is also markedly different from that of more wealthy advanced countries such as the United States. (See Table 7.2.) The difference in the general pat-

TABLE 7.2. Structure of Investment,
U.S. and U.S.S.R.
(per cent of total)

	U.S.	U.S.S.R.	
	1963	1952	1962
Industry	35.5	45.5	39.3
Agriculture	3.7	13.7	16.0
Housing	24.6	19.4	19.2
Trade, Education and Other Services*	22.8	12.3	16.5
Transportation and Communication	13.3	9.1	9.0

* Includes municipal economy

tern is most strikingly seen in the distribution between the top and the bottom half of the table. The Russians have directed well over half of all investment into industry and agriculture compared with less than 40 per cent for the United States. This was made possible by their restraint in investing in housing, in facilities to provide such services as health and education, and in urban amenities. They have also directed a substantially smaller share into transportation, primarily by avoiding the construction of the elaborate kind of highway system that has required such large resources in our country. The high share of investment which the Russians devote to agriculture is somewhat surprising, considering how they have consistently tried to limit the claims of agriculture in order to conserve resources for high-priority industrial investment. But the agricultural sector is so large and the productivity of resources in it so low that they have still had to allocate a much larger share of the total to agriculture than we do. There have been some important changes in the Soviet investment allocation in the last decade, bringing it closer to our own. In the early fifties the share of industry was appreciably higher than it is now. The programs which Khrushchev sponsored to improve agricultural performance meant a redistribution away from industry toward agriculture. Even taken together, however, industry and agriculture have lost ground in the post-Stalin years to the consumer-oriented service sectors.

Overall, the Soviet investment program has probably had a relatively low *capital intensity*. It has emphasized activities, such as industry, in which the rubles' worth of investment required to raise GNP by one ruble is relatively low and has avoided activities, such as housing, in which the payoff in incremental output is smaller. The lower the capital output ratio, the larger the increment in aggregate output one can obtain from a given flow of investment resources. With investment the bottleneck sector in Soviet development, low capital intensity has enhanced the "growth effectiveness" of investment. The Russian planners have enjoyed the advantage of a relatively low capital output ratio just because of the nature of the things they wanted to do. Their main objective was industrialization, and industry is a sector of the economy where the capital output ratio is relatively low. Also they have tried to keep the capital output ratio for their total investment program as low as possible by sidestepping investment in the highly capital-intensive sectors of the economy. The most striking examples of this policy are found in the planners' attitudes toward housing and transportation. In the case of housing, they have permitted the amount of space per urban dweller to fall during nearly the whole period of industrialization. As industrialization proceeded and people flocked to the cities, the Soviet regime did not add housing space at a proportional rate. Rather, the planners permitted only a modest program of housing construction so that more and more people were crowded into the existing housing space. Housing was treated as a low-priority investment, and when materials, labor, or other resources were in short supply, it was housing which was sacrificed rather than other types of investment. Characteristically, the housing plans were unfulfilled. Not until the sixties did the average living space available for the urban inhabitant regain even the point at which it had stood in 1926 before forced industrialization began. And that was in any case a wretchedly low level —

less than 6 square meters (about 64 square feet) per person compared with a figure of about 200 square feet in the U.S. The Russians have also tried to keep the capital output ratio low and avoid additional investment in many sectors by constantly intensifying their use of the capital stocks inherited from the prerevolutionary period. How this has worked in transportation and some other uses will be discussed further below.

National Income by Sector of Origin

It is also instructive to look at the distribution of national income by sector of origin, to ask what portion of it was generated in industry, agriculture, and so on. A comparison of the United States and U.S.S.R. in this respect is shown in Table 7.3. The most remark-

TABLE 7.3. National Income by
Sector of Origin
(per cent of total)

	U.S. 1963	U.S.S.R. 1962
Industry	32.1	36
Construction	5.2	6.9
Agriculture	4.0	26.6
Transportation	4.1	5.1
Communications	2	.7
Domestic Trade	16.3	4.4
Other Service	36.3	20.2

able difference between the Soviet GNP seen in this light and the GNP in more advanced countries is agriculture's high share in the U.S.S.R. Although the Russians have come a long way in the effort to industrialize, a very large share of the total population is still engaged in agriculture, and agriculture still accounts for over twenty-five per cent of the total output of the economy, compared with only four per cent in the United States. Two separate reasons account for this difference. In the United States, high productivity in agriculture has made it possible to divert the preponderance of American resources into activities other than the primary one of feeding ourselves. Second, high productivity in our farm operations makes the relative cost of agricultural products quite low, so that even though our agricultural output is large in physical volume, its value in relation to the total output of the economy is further depressed. That so high a share of Soviet GNP should be generated by agriculture reflects the inability of the Soviet system thus far to realize analogous gains in agricultural productivity. Note also that the Russians devote a somewhat greater fraction of their resources to construction and to the provision of transportation services.

Paradoxically, considering how much of its resources the U.S.S.R. must allocate to keep itself fed, the share of income created in industry is also higher than is the comparable share of United States income. The explanation of this paradox is an extension of the argument already cited. In the United States high productivity in industry and agriculture means that our requirements for the outputs of these activities can be met with far less than all our resources and we can afford to devote the rest to providing a varied multitude of services. The service sector of the economy, producing such items as education, health, conveniences to the consumer, recreation, and so on, is where the much poorer Russians have had to skimp in comparison with our pattern of resource use.

How Big Is Soviet GNP?

A central issue in any evaluation of Soviet capabilities and achievements is how large the output of the Soviet economy has gotten to be. But that issue is much complicated by the problem of finding an appropriate yardstick. The figure of 153.71 billion rubles for Soviet GNP in 1958 cited in Table 7.1 is meaningless by itself. The real issue is how much output that represents compared with the output of the American or of some other economy with which we are familiar. In trying to answer this question, we find ourselves confronted once again with the index number problem. It is easy enough to answer questions about the relative size of Soviet output if one limits his attention to very small portions of the total. For instance, it would be easy, subject to some problems of quality differences, to state the size of Soviet shoe production or bread production compared with the American output of the same commodities. There are statistical, but no conceptual, difficulties in answering the question of how many miles of new railroad track were created as part of the investment program of each country in a given year. Imagine for the moment that one can make this kind of comparison in physical terms for each different kind of good or service that entered into the various end-use categories considered above in Table 7.1. The resulting ratios of Soviet to American output would vary greatly from item to item. The Russians produce a much smaller amount of nearly every consumer good than we do, although for some — like potatoes, cabbage, or rye bread — they probably produce more. The indexes of Soviet output compared with ours in this area would range from 0 (for sugar-coated breakfast cereals, say) to several hundred for bread, though in general the ratios for consumer goods would tend to be quite low.

For other end-uses it would frequently be found that Soviet output was much closer to, and occasionally larger than, ours. The number of bricks produced and used for investment purposes and the number of certain kinds of machines added to the Soviet capital stock each year, for instance, is probably greater than in the United States. Similarly, the volume of inputs used for military purposes in the Soviet Union would be found to exceed United States expenditures in some cases — manpower being the most striking example. Although the annual amounts of most hardware items procured for the Soviet armed forces would be smaller than ours, we would find the Russians much closer to us here than in the flow of passenger automobiles being produced for the population.

Any answer to "How big is Soviet output compared with U.S. output overall?" can be thought of as the result of striking some sort of average for all these relative output ratios. (Remember that earlier the rate of growth for industrial output was described as an average for the rates of growth for many separate components of industrial output.) An index number problem emerges here, just as in the case of growth measurements, because there exist alternative weighting systems for computing this average. If the American price system, for example, is used to weight the separate output ratios, Soviet output appears to be a relatively large fraction of ours but if the ratios are weighted by Soviet prices, the Russians seem to be very much farther behind on the average. Weighting by dollar prices gives an answer which is equivalent to that which would be gotten by adding up all the elements of Soviet output at the dollar prices placed on them in our economy and comparing the resulting total with United States GNP in dollars. Ruble weighting is equivalent to comparing Soviet output with what United States output would sum to if each element were counted in at the ruble prices prevailing in the Soviet economy. In a calculation made for 1955, it was found that ruble weighting showed Soviet GNP as about one-fourth as big as United States GNP but dollar weighting made it a little over half as much as ours. Similar calculations are not available for more recent years but the price and output structures of the two countries remain sufficiently different so that a comparison made for 1963 would show a similarly distressing ambiguity.

Which of these answers is right? The basic similarity of this problem to the earlier index number problem related to growth suggests that the answer depends on first clarifying what is meant by the question — "How big is Soviet output relative to ours?" Without going into all the complexities of the argument here, we may simply assert that in this case either extreme is probably misleading and some sort of average between the two alternatives is likely to make more economic sense. The difficulty is that our yardstick of the relative importance of different commodities, i.e., their relative prices, has no inherent fixity. How valuable a given item is in relation to another depends on their relative scarcity or abundance and it makes little sense to pretend that the low relative prices on some United States goods would persist in a situation where these goods were relatively much less abundant.

The most sensible way of coping with the index number problem in this area is to reformulate our question to make it more specific. The larger the aggregates considered and the more general the question about relative size, the greater will be the index number ambiguity. The spread between the two answers is greater for GNP than it is when we narrow the area under consideration and ask about the amount of Soviet *consumption* relative to United States consumption. Actually, when one asks about the size of Soviet GNP, he usually has in the back of his mind some more precise motive. He would like to know, for instance, how well Soviet consumers fare compared with American citizens or how large a military effort the Russians are making compared with our own. By reformulating the question in this more specific and narrow way, one can reduce the index number ambiguity somewhat. Looked at in this way, the answers turn out to be something as follows. The Soviet Union is very, very, very far behind the United States in terms of the amount of consumption goods produced and, because of their larger population, still farther behind in terms of per capita consumption. In other important uses, however, ones which are really much more relevant to issues of international image making and military rivalry, the Soviet Union is much closer. For example, they probably spend nearly as much resources as we do in the area of creating and maintaining their military strength and also in the area of investment — on which, of course, the growth performance of an economy is very dependent. They probably have a larger industrial investment program than we do, although because of the different structure of their investment pattern their total investment program is smaller. One still faces the problem of averaging these separate estimates into an overall evaluation of the competitive position of the Russians in the struggle for international prestige and power but in this weighting one can probably find better criteria of relative importance than relative prices.

Productivity of Resources

The Soviet Union is a big country, possessing tremendous natural and population resources. In addition the allocation policy described above has enabled it to accumulate during the past 35 years a stock of capital of impressive size. The scale of its resource endowment puts it, along with the United States, in the select company of economic superpowers. In 1963 the total labor force in the United States consisted of 68.8 million persons (distributed 63.9 million in the nonfarm sector and 4.9 million in agriculture). In the Soviet Union, employment in the nonfarm economy in 1963 was nearly as large as ours (62.1 million persons) and there were an additional 30 million persons engaged in agriculture, to put them far ahead of us with respect to total labor force. As will be seen below, the amount of other resources devoted to agriculture is also very large.

It is in the area of capital stock that the Soviet relative resource position is poorest. This is especially true of capital in such service activities as housing, general urban improvements, trade and distribution. In terms of "productive" capital, such as factories, railroad rolling stock, etc., the Russians are much closer. Capital is probably the most difficult of all resources to measure but if we simply take the ruble value of the Soviet national wealth and convert it at a reasonable ruble-dollar ratio in order to approximate what dollar value might have been placed on all those items of equipment if they had been produced in the United States, the Soviet capital stock appears to be only about a third as large as ours. Economists sometimes try to aggregate all of these different kinds of inputs to derive an overall measure of resource inputs in the two countries, though this is probably a more or less fruitless exercise. In addition to very difficult problems of comparability and measurement of individual resources, there is the ever-present index number problem as well. Any assessment of overall resource productivity must be an extremely tenuous exercise, and highly variable conclusions have been drawn by different authors. We will be content to assert here that the relatively high standing of the U.S.S.R. on all these comparisons of resource input, together with their relatively small output compared with ours, obviously implies a very much lower productivity for resources in the Soviet economy. This in turn is a powerful indication that there are great inefficiencies in the Soviet system.

This kind of macro-economic comparison of productivity only suggests how serious the problem of productivity is for the Russians and does not really tell very much about *why* the productivity of Soviet resources is so low. Much more interesting and useful in this respect are individual productivity comparisons. Examination of individual cases will make it easier to understand why the Russians tend to get less output per unit of input, and will also show interesting differences in productivity from sector to sector. In some sectors and in the use of some kinds of resources the Russians do nearly as well as we do but in others their productivity is incredibly low.

Before starting on this survey of Soviet resource productivity, it should be made clear that productivity is not the same thing as efficiency. The impossibility of equating the two directly is related to the following circumstance. Frequently the different inputs into some product are partly substitutable for each other. A given amount of output can usually be made with less labor if the producer is willing to use more electricity; the input of coke per ton of pig iron can be reduced by using more expensive and complicated equipment. There are many different recipes for the production of a given output and the proportions between ingredients vary from recipe to recipe. Consequently the efficient thing for a country to do is to pick recipes which utilize more of the resources which the country has in abundance and which economize on those resources that are scarce. So if it is found that the ratio of the input of one ingredient to some output in Soviet economy is high or low compared with what it is in the United States, this is not conclusive proof that the cook has been either wasteful or efficient. But, even taking into account this danger, the consideration of productivity ratios will still be extremely instructive. In many processes the possibilities of substitution are limited. Another thing that can be done is to give particular attention to the productivity of the scarcest resource which in the Soviet economy is generally capital.

Equipment Productivity. Equipment productivity can be taken as a kind of surrogate for capital productivity. By comparing with American performance the amount of output which the Russians get from a given amount of productive equipment in some process, we get an idea of how effectively they are using their scarcest resource. For many processes it is difficult to find a way of summing up in a single indicator the amount of equipment that is being used. A factory producing tractors, for instance, uses many different kinds of machines and there is no way to add them all together in a single measure of equipment, except in value terms. Moreover, in many industries output consists of many different kinds of products and there is no physical common denominator to which all the outputs can be converted. In such cases international comparisons of equipment productivity are almost impossible. But in a number of processes there are more or less satisfactory physical measures both for equipment and output so that output per unit of equipment in the United States and the Soviet Union can be compared.

One example is found in railroad transportation. The output of any form of transportation has two main dimensions — the amount of freight carried and the average distance that each ton is carried. So it is customary to express the output of transportation in terms of the "ton-mile," the work involved in hauling one ton of freight one mile. Consider the inputs required to provide transportation; there are labor, fuel, repair, and, very important in the case of railroads, a large capital stock. This capital includes rolling stock — freight cars and locomotives, and a big investment in roadbed — tracks, ties, bridges, signaling devices, etc. Transportation is distinguished by the very heavy investment in this kind of capital required per dollar's worth of transportation produced. Hence an important productivity measure in rail transport is the intensity of utilization of this capital investment or, looked at the other way round, the output per unit of capital stock.

A comparison of railroad output with the stock of freight cars and with the miles of track operated generates two interesting partial measures of capital productivity in this sector of the economy. In 1963 the total freight turnover on the Soviet railroads of 1,221 billion ton-miles was produced with a stock of freight cars that aggregated 45–50 million tons of carrying capacity for a productivity of 21–24 thousand ton-miles per ton of capacity. In the United States in 1963, the output was only about 7.2 thousand ton-miles per ton of freight car capacity. The implication of this difference in productivity is that the Russians were able to do a given transportation job with only a third as many freight cars as were required on American railroads.

The same sort of calculation can be made for intensity of utilization of the roadbed of the Soviet railroad system. In 1956 the length of first main track on Soviet railroads was 80 thousand miles. With turnover of 1,221 billion ton-miles, freight haulage per mile of railroad track was almost 15 million ton-miles. In the United States this ratio was only 2.9 million ton-miles per mile of track. The Russians manage to perform a given amount of transportation with less than a fourth of the length of railroad employed in the United States.

The low American figures result in part from the fact that we overbuilt our railroads at one stage of our economic development. As later forms of transportation have developed and taken freight away from the railroads, trackage and the number of freight cars on hand has declined much more slowly so that the productivity indicators worsened. Also the economies in rolling stock and railroad trackage which the Russians have managed to secure involve some extra costs at other points in the economy. For example, when the railroads are overcrowded, this means slow and uncertain railroad service which prompts industrial managers to hoard inventories of materials. So the economy of investment in railroad line and rolling stock is partly offset by excessive investment in inventories elsewhere in the economy.

In the iron and steel industry, one of the most important units of equipment is the blast furnace in which iron ore is converted to pig iron. Blast furnaces vary greatly in size so that the total amount of blast furnace capacity cannot be measured just by the number of blast furnaces. But it is possible to use as a measure of capacity the aggregate volume of all blast furnaces, that is, the total inside space in which the work of a blast furnace is performed. This capacity can be related to the output of pig iron from blast furnaces to give a measure of blast furnace productivity. When this indicator is compared for the United States and the Soviet Union, it turns out that the Russians use their blast furnaces much more intensely than American companies — the Soviet figure is about 1.40 tons of pig iron per cubic meter of blast furnace capacity per day as against about one ton per cubic meter per day for American furnaces. This relatively higher performance of Soviet furnaces is all the more surprising when it is realized that American furnaces are larger on the average than Soviet furnaces. Larger furnaces are usually more productive per cubic meter of volume than smaller furnaces, so one might expect American productivity to be higher because of this fact alone, but the difference is in the other direction. If the Russians obtained only the American levels of performance from their blast furnaces, they would have needed 160 blast furnaces to produce as much pig iron as they did rather than the 120 or so they actually had in the early sixties. So it is obvious that the resources saved by higher equipment productivity are great enough to make a real contribution to economic growth.

Equipment productivity is not always higher in the Soviet Union than in the United States. In the cotton textile industry, for instance, the statistics indicate that Russian producers do rather less well than American. In the spinning branch of the industry, they are about on a par with us, but in cotton goods weaving,

Soviet output per loom per hour is only about 60 per cent as large as the American ratio. This difference in productivity is undoubtedly due to the fact that the Soviet equipment is older and less advanced technologically than the corresponding machinery in the United States. In cotton weaving in particular, the Soviet Union has a much smaller proportion of automatic looms than United States industry does. As an industry serving consumer needs, the Soviet textile industry has been treated as a step-child of the industrialization, so to speak, and has not had the same care lavished on its technology as higher priority branches of industry have. But this case illustrates an important aspect of equipment use in the Soviet economy. The Russians manage pretty well to make up for the poor productivity of their equipment by working it longer hours than United States firms do. Thus if one considers output per loom *per year* rather than *per hour of operation,* the spread between American and Soviet productivity is much less. Compensating for the relative backwardness of their equipment by more intensive utilization is probably characteristic throughout the Soviet economy.

Labor Productivity. The Russians claim to have achieved a level of output per worker in industry of 40–50 per cent of that in the United States. This is probably something of an exaggeration since it depends essentially on accepting their claim about relative size of industrial output. A look at some individual cases will provide a better idea of what Soviet labor productivity really is and also reveal some clues as to why productivity is low.

Coal mining is one of the industries in which the Russians show up least well. In 1963 average output per man per day in Soviet mines was 2.1 metric tons compared with over 14 tons in United States mines. Why? Several possible explanations come to mind. Knowing from our own experience how much higher productivity is in strip mines than in underground mines, one wonders if the Russians are disadvantaged in having fewer open mines. Actually the share is about the same — 30 per cent of Soviet and 31 per cent of American coal is produced from open pit mines. But it is interesting to find that the Russians are much less backward in strip mines (with labor productivity equal to 44 per cent of ours) than in underground mines (where it is equal to only 15 per cent).

With our attention thus focussed on underground mines, we might ask about differences in the geological conditions under which coal is mined. With regard to the average depth at which coal lies and the thickness of seams mined, the Russians probably *are* in a worse situation. As the following tabulation shows, the Russians get a considerably larger share of their output from relatively thin seams, and the fact that they get a larger share from some very thick seams does not really offset this disadvantage.

	Per cent of coal mined	
Seam thickness	U.S.	U.S.S.R.
Up to 4 ft.	31.3	47.3
4–6 ft.	36.4	24.0
6–8 ft.	24.4	7.9
8 ft. and over	8.9	20.8

Perhaps the Russians have not yet achieved American levels of mechanization — the rise in output per miner in the United States in the last several decades owes much to increases in the capital equipment that supplements the miner's power. To pursue that argument reveals a paradox. Horsepower of equipment per miner does turn out to be much less for Soviet than for American coal miners but in relation to *output* the Russians have as much horsepower as we do! What would happen if enough Soviet miners were eliminated to bring their horsepower-per-worker ratio up to the American level? We may be properly suspicious of the argument that because each miner now had as much power to work with as his American counterpart he would display the same productivity. The suspicion rests on the probability that the horsepower in Soviet coal mining is scattered among and embodied in a stock of equipment that requires a large labor force to operate it. In other words, the explanation for low labor productivity is the inefficient and obsolete technology embodied in the capital stock. (This kind of situation is probably a very common one in the Soviet economy.) Even with all these elements for an explanation of low labor productivity in coal mining, it seems likely that, in order to account for the poor Russian showing, a large allowance would have to be added for poor organization, planning, and motivation.

A comparison of labor productivity in steel shows the Russians in a much more favorable light. The steel industry covers a succession of processes — the production of pig iron, its conversion into steel, and the processing of steel ingots into rolled shapes of varying degrees of fabrication. Overall, the Soviet steel industry shows a lower degree of fabrication than the United States industry. A higher share of Soviet pig iron is consumed in castings without conversion to steel and a higher share of their steel is cast than rolled. But let us assume that measuring output at an intermediate point in the process — i.e., in terms of the tons of steel tapped from steel furnaces — provides an adequate measure of relative size. If we look at it this way, the Russian output is 81 per cent of the American output but they use 1.73 times the manpower, so their output per worker is 47 per cent of ours. (These figures refer to 1963.) This much better performance compared with coal is due to the fact that steel is a higher priority industry which has been given advantages in investment and research, and, as a result, technological progress has been faster. That the Russians are as far behind in labor productivity as they are is largely due to the fact that this modernization has affected primarily the main processes, such as blast furnace operation, while many auxiliary operations within the steel mill, such as repair, materials handling, transportation, and others, are still carried on with older, labor-intensive technologies.

Petroleum refining is an intermediate case. In 1963 the Russians refined 152 million tons of crude oil with a labor force of 97 thousand men, while U.S. refineries refined 427 million tons with a labor force of 95 thousand — so that Russian labor productivity was about one-third of ours. Actually this exaggerates the Russian position since they process crude oil much less intensively. The Russians get a much lower yield of gasoline and more residuals because they employ less widely the complicated refining processes such as cracking and hydrofining, and produce a much lower quality product as measured by sulfur content, octane numbers, and other indicators. The explanation for low productivity runs in terms of old-fashioned refinery design. The Soviet planners have built their units and plants on too small a scale. The plants are spread over excessive areas so that they are awkward to man. There is too little automation and too much manual measuring and operation of valves. Their own discussions acknowledge that they made the foolish mistake of pouring tremendous investments into refineries of obsolete design when the experience of other countries had already evolved much more efficient ones.

The above examples could be supplemented with many others but the general features that they reveal would be changed little. We would continue to find considerable variation in comparative labor productivity from industry to industry, with the explanation turning on differences in the priority given to technical upgrading, in the inherent resource situation, and in the timing of the growth pattern (which in turn has influenced how fast the Russians could embody improved technology in the capital stock of the industry). Qualitative differences in the labor force surely account for some of the difference in productivity. The general level of skill is probably less in the Soviet than in the American labor force and there is a higher proportion of women. And in the last analysis, the explanation of the low output per worker in the U.S.S.R. usually also contains a large ingredient of distorted incentives, errors of economic calculation, and other weaknesses of planning.

At a somewhat deeper level of analysis, however, the most important reason for low labor productivity is that the Russians are using lavishly the resource that they have in greatest abundance. When capital is the bottleneck factor but there is plenty of labor, as is the case in the Soviet economy, it is rational to substitute labor for capital, even though this means high labor input per unit of output. Planners in charge of designing plants will find it advisable to use production techniques that save on capital, even though they may require extra labor, and once the plants are built managers will try to meet their output goals by using them as intensively as possible. The system of incentives has traditionally emphasized output more than cost, and when managers have a choice, they will try to meet output goals by crowding more labor into a given plant. The era of easy expansion of the labor force is now passing, however. The Russians are not now able to keep increasing the nonagricultural labor force as fast as they could in the past. But one should be wary of the conclusion that the Russians are so wasteful of labor that its supply will constitute an obstacle to their ever catching up with us in total output. Even if the additions to the Soviet labor force characteristic of the past are no longer possible in the future, large increments of output can now be obtained by concentrating on increasing output per worker.

Material Input Ratios.   A third kind of input-output ratio that illuminates some aspects of efficiency is the expenditure of material or fuel per unit of output. How much final output can be gotten from a given amount of primary resources to satisfy final demands depends in part on how much of the intermediate output is wasted along the way.

A striking illustration of this point is found in the electric power generating industry. The electric power industry is engaged essentially in transforming the heat energy of various kinds of fuels into electric energy. Both input and output in this case are subject to fairly precise physical measurement, the fuel input in terms of heat content (BTU or calories) and the electric power produced in terms of kilowatt-hours. The ratio of these two magnitudes is one of the most commonly used indicators of the performance of electric power plants. In 1963, the fuel expenditure of Soviet power stations was 12,167 BTU per thousand KWH, whereas in the United States the input ratio was 10,444 BTU per thousand KWH. This ratio provides a good overall index of the level of technical development of a country's power industry. It depends on the size of electric power generating units, on the temperatures and pressures at which steam is used, and on the general technical level of equipment used. The Soviet Union has a higher fuel consumption because it has failed to take advantage of these possibilities of economizing fuel to the same extent as the United States has. The waste of resources which this difference in performance involves is clearly seen in the following calculation. If the Soviet fuel input per kilowatt-hour of electric power produced had been as low as that in the United States, the Soviets would have saved the equivalent of 29 million tons of coal in 1963 which would be over 5 per cent of their total actual production of coal.

Another interesting example of Soviet wastefulness is the utilization of raw material in the machinery industry. The machine building industry is engaged essentially in shaping and fabricating metal by a variety of processes. One of the main processes involved in making most machines — lathes, turbines, automobiles, or any other — is shaping and forming metal. Raw metal stock is melted and cast into shapes, and stamped or forged, and machined on boring, milling, or other metal cutting machines to make the parts that go into the final product. In the process metal is trimmed away in the form of chips and shavings, ends and bits sheared off, and the metal left when blanks are stamped from a sheet. In the Soviet machinery industry the ratio of scrap to the original input is 23 per cent, whereas in the United States it is only about 19 per cent. There are several reasons for this high ratio. (1) The Russians do too much casting in comparison with other processes like stamping. When metal is cast it can be shaped only roughly to the dimensions required of the finished piece and the excess of metal must later be trimmed away. Moreover, the Russians tend to use casting methods that are less precise than others that could be used. (2) Soviet machinery plants frequently find it very difficult to obtain the assortment of sizes and dimensions of metal they want. The metal producers prefer to make large sizes with excess tolerances since this makes it easier for them to fulfill their output plans. But this means that the machinery industry must spend extra effort in making big pieces into little pieces. Given the need to make a part a given size, the only available stock may be much larger than required and so it will have to be machined down excessively. (3) The managers of machinery plants are just careless — they do not take care to minimize the metal input in the way they should. They will not be judged severely on this aspect of their behavior and so they do not worry about it.

The metal itself is not necessarily wasted since the shavings and chips are collected and returned to the iron and steel industry, eventually to re-emerge as new metal. But this reworking is wasteful in itself and the machinery industry is forced to spend far too much machine time, electrical power, and the time of machine operators on the process of cutting away unwanted metal.

Excessive expenditure of metal per unit of output is quite common in the Soviet economy. Any Soviet machinery item, such as a truck, a lathe, or a locomotive, is likely to be heavier than a western model of equivalent capacity because of inefficient design. In the construction of oil and gas wells the Russians use more pipe per well than the rest of the world's drillers and the explanation is quite characteristic. Savings in metal expenditure have been made elsewhere in the world because improvements in strength have permitted the oil industry to use thinner wall pipe both for drilling and casing. Also the development of special equipment has made it possible to test wells before casing them and therefore avoid the waste of casing dry holes. But given the unresponsiveness of Soviet producers to the wishes of their customers, Russian oil men have not been able to get this kind of improved equipment from their suppliers and so are forced to be less economical than they could be.

However, Soviet performance on materials consumption is not everywhere as bad as in these examples. Another very important fuel-using sector is the iron and steel industry, both in the blast furnaces in which iron ore is reduced to pig iron and in the open-hearth furnaces in which the pig iron is refined to steel. Fuel consumption in blast furnaces in the two economies is almost the same — 0.683 tons of coke per ton of pig iron produced in the United States and 0.690 tons in the Soviet Union in 1962. Finally, it is possible to find occasional instances where the Russians achieve equally good or even slightly better ratios of output to raw material than we do. Nevertheless, the indicators we have described probably suggest the correct generalization, namely, that the Russians tend to be wasteful of material inputs. Their performance as between different sectors is rather uneven but on the average it is less good than that of the United States economy.

Agriculture.   The examples given so far all relate to the non-agricultural sectors of the economy. Agriculture is a special case, probably the most inefficient branch of the Soviet economy, and it merits separate consideration. The collective farm system, at least in the form in which it has existed in the Soviet Union until recently, has clearly been a very ineffective institution for stimulating efficiency or technical progress in agriculture. As was suggested in Chapter 2, this way of organizing agriculture was really adopted more for its virtue as a means of forcing tribute from the peasants than for its ability to stimulate agricultural production. The statistics show that it has indeed failed in the latter role; over most of the period of Soviet industrialization the collective farm system has offered an insuperable obstacle to improvements in productive efficiency. The main exception to this generalization was in the first five years after Stalin's death, when important innovations in agriculture achieved a significant, if short-lived, spurt in the productivity of agricultural resources.

As indicated above, the Soviet agricultural labor force is roughly six times that of the United States. Soviet agriculture also employs much more land — total crop land harvested in the United States in 1963 was 293 million acres and in the Soviet Union 540 million acres. (This is not the only kind of agricultural land and the Russians are somewhat less well supplied with pasture and grazing land than the United States — 500 million acres compared with our 694 million acres.) The stock of farm animals in the Soviet Union nearly equals United States numbers. The Russians have fewer head of cattle (about 85.4 million versus 106.1 million on January 1, 1964 and these are more concentrated on milk animals than beef cattle). On the other hand, they have more than four times as many sheep and goats. The Soviet swine population has fluctuated widely but in recent years has exceeded ours. With these resources, however, the Soviet Union produces a considerably smaller agricultural output. Because weather causes big fluctuations from year to year, it is meaningless to compare crop production in a single year but averages for the most recent five years (1959–63) show the following results. There are a few crops in which the Russians have the larger output — Soviet potato output is four times ours and sugar beet output is several times larger. The Russians also produce considerable amounts of sunflower seed for vegetable oil and flax for linen, while the United States has no significant production of these crops. (There are, of course, several important crops which we produce but they do not, such as sugar cane.) But in the really important products they are far behind — Soviet grain production is only about two-thirds of American, cotton 45 per cent, fruits one-third, and vegetables 75 per cent. In animal products they are behind us, except in milk where they are about even. Meat production is 70 per cent and eggs less than half of ours. (Each of these ratios should probably be discounted somewhat because of exaggerations in the Soviet output figure. Also in thinking about this in terms of consumption, it should be remembered that the Soviet population is about 227 million versus a United States population of 190 million in the early sixties but that a much larger share of United States agricultural output is exported.) Considering the relative importance of these different kinds of produce, it is clear that aggregate Soviet output is far smaller than ours.

The contrast between the relative standings in output and resource input obviously implies very low comparative productivity of resources in Soviet agriculture and examination of detailed productivity ratios bears this out. Crop yields — output per unit of land — in Soviet agriculture are very low. Grain yields are less than half the United States figures and for potatoes and sugar beets yields are only one-third as high. The overall yield for cotton is about the same but the Russians produce almost exclusively irrigated cotton which shows appreciably higher yields than cotton grown without irrigation. Compared with irrigated areas in the United States, Soviet output per acre is only half as large. It is significant that cotton is the one crop that has generally been paid for by the state at a price approximating its cost of production rather than at the confiscatory prices paid for most other farm produce.

Yields in animal husbandry (which represent a kind of capital-output ratio) are equally low. Soviet cows produce only a little over half as much milk per year as American cows, and the number of eggs produced per chicken is much lower. There are interesting differences in milk yield between socialized and private plot agriculture. Average production per privately owned cow in 1963 was 1,706 pounds per year but for the cows owned by state and collective farms only 1,517 pounds. Though probably poorer in terms of breed, the privately owned cows are better cared for. The U.S.S.R. has a very small meat production, considering the size of its animal herds. The explanation is that Soviet animals are of poor quality, they are not fed properly to make them gain weight rapidly, and slaughter weights are low.

The explanation for the low productivity of resources in agriculture is complicated. The explanation is partly the unfavorable natural conditions of Soviet agriculture. In terms of growing season, rainfall, temperatures, soil fertility, etc., the Russians are at a serious disadvantage compared with American farmers. One reason for the high American grain yield is that corn is an important element in the grain economy and corn has a yield per acre several times that of wheat. The Russians have very limited area where they can grow corn to maturity and nothing like the

United States corn belt. Their wheat yields are low because over much of their wheat area a short growing season interferes with both planting and harvesting and there is insufficient moisture. Low labor productivity can be explained partly by the fact that Russian agriculture has always been stinted on mechanical equipment and other capital. The Russians have about 922 thousand trucks on farms, whereas we have nearly three million. They have about a million and a half tractors, whereas American agriculture has over 4.5 million. Soviet investment priorities have always restricted investment in agriculture to conserve these resources for other sectors.

But low productivity must also be explained to a large extent as the result of the system. Soviet agricultural policies and institutions have been a serious obstacle to improvements in productivity. In most of the rest of the world, and especially in the United States, agriculture has been a very dynamic sector in the last two decades, a sector in which truly spectacular rises in productivity have been achieved. Yields per acre, per animal, per manhour have risen consistently and dramatically. The present high productivity of resources in American farming is due to rapid technological progress of diverse forms — the use of better equipment, the introduction of better seed varieties and animal breeds, the discovery of more efficient ways of organizing agricultural production, the use of fertilizer, chemical means for pest control, etc. These innovations are the result of an elaborate system of government sponsored agricultural research, a system for disseminating knowledge of new techniques, crops, and methods; and a motivation to implant the improvements at the working level. Soviet agriculture, in the 35 years since collectivization, has done a wretched job of adopting these innovations and so has not moved much beyond the premodern levels of productivity that it had already attained before collectivization. One careful study concluded that the productivity of resources in Soviet agriculture actually declined in the prewar period and rose virtually not at all over the whole period from 1928 to Stalin's death in 1953. The Soviet collective farm system and central planning of agriculture have hampered the introduction of better methods and have choked off progress.

At the time of Stalin's death, the Russians had come to a real impasse in agriculture — the technique of exploitation could not well be pushed further and any increases in agricultural output demanded improvements in agricultural productivity. The next five years was a period of considerable improvement. The present situation regarding productivity, bad as it seems, represents a great improvement over a decade ago. The core of the reform was to give the collective farmers more incentive by raising prices, to give them more control over farm operations by dissolving the machine tractor stations, to make studies of costs as a guide to better regional specialization, and to make it possible for investment in agriculture to increase. This attack on some of the basic difficulties was accompanied by a crash program to break the output bottleneck by an expansion of sown acreage in the virgin lands program. Between 1954 and 1961 the Russians plowed up around 100 million acres of land in Kazakstan and Western Siberia not formerly cropped and planted it to wheat. (This is double the United States wheat acreage and represents an expansion in Soviet acreage of about one-fourth.) This was something of a gamble, since the area is characterized by a deficiency of moisture and dustbowl tendencies, but it paid off handsomely as a short run measure to cope with the grain crisis while allowing a breathing space for a more fundamental attack on the problem of farm efficiency. After 1958, as a result of downgrading agriculture once again and of bad weather, especially drought in the virgin lands, the growth of output and productivity faltered and the Russians returned to the brink of agricultural disaster. But the post-Khrushchev leadership seems to have acknowledged to themselves the importance of measures to improve agriculture and there may be another period of rapid improvement in prospect.

Implications of Productivity Findings. What conclusions about the efficiency or wastefulness of the Soviet economy are to be drawn from this survey of productivity ratios? Several generalizations summarize briefly what has been found.

1. First, as between the different kinds of productivity, the Russians generally have fairly high capital equipment productivity and low labor productivity. This is what we would expect, given the relative availability of capital and labor in the Soviet economy.

2. The ratios of material and fuel input per unit of output tend

to be rather higher than the corresponding figures for the United States. This kind of indicator is much less likely to be influenced by the differences in factor endowment than the capital and labor productivity figures and so the relatively poor performance we found here must surely reflect carelessness in organization and errors in technological policy.

3. The productivity of all resources in agriculture is very low. With so many people working in agriculture, the Russians ought to have much higher crop yields and higher output per animal than we do. American yields are actually fairly low compared with those in many countries. A relative abundance of land and paucity of labor in the United States have combined to encourage a pattern of farming in which we use a little labor on a large expanse of land, with the result that output per unit of land is less than it would be if land were used more intensely. Nevertheless yields are much higher in American than in Soviet agriculture.

4. Finally, even when only a single kind of productivity indicator is considered, there is great variability from industry to industry. This heterogeneity suggests imbalance and unevenness in planning. It seems a clear conclusion that the Russians have been slower to take advantage of technological progress and organizational improvements in some branches than in others and that the Soviet system of incentives and controls has been much more effective in some sectors of the economy than in others in getting managers and planners to improve performance. There is also an implication here that capital investment planning has been faulty. One suspects that the planners have not always directed their investment to the areas where it would have the greatest effect in raising labor productivity and reducing manpower requirements.

Taken together, all these productivity indicators suggest that the Soviet economy is less efficient in getting output from the available resources than is the American economy. At the same time, the findings should warn us to keep a sense of proportion. They certainly do not support the notion that the Soviet economy is so wasteful that in the long run it cannot compete economically with the capitalist economies of the western world. After all, the productivity comparisons throughout have been with levels of performance in the United States which are generally the highest in the world. For many of the indicators described, Soviet performance would be above the levels achieved by the industrialized capitalist countries of Western Europe.

Finally, we should note that there is a second meaning implicit in most of the productivity indicators examined. Throughout the chapter emphasis has been laid on the idea that the figures show that the Russians generally get less output per unit of resources employed than we do but, equally important, they imply that the Russians have great possibilities for improvement. There is an amusing difference in vocabulary between Soviet and western discussions of their productivity. What we label waste, they call "reserves." This is partly the typical Soviet predilection for euphemisms to describe sore spots but there is more to it than that. In many cases low productivity indicators represent more the present stage of Soviet industrialization than any inherent inefficiency in their economic system. As time passes, big improvements in many of these productivity ratios can be expected, and it can indeed be shown that many kinds of productivity are rising more rapidly in the Soviet economy than in the American. This means that the Soviet leaders can look forward to great possibilities for economic growth just by improving productivity. Even if there should be a slowdown in the rate at which they can expand their capital, their labor force, and the area they use for agriculture, there are potential offsets in productivity increases and possibilities of getting more output from a given amount of resources.

8

Prospects for the Future

Birth certificate

Having analyzed Russian economic performance and explored the
relationship of this performance to Soviet economic institutions,
we are now ready to engage in some speculation about the future
of the Soviet economy and of its rivalry with the United States.
Basically the question concerns relative rates of growth. If the
Soviet Union continues to expand output at more rapid rates than
we do, the implications for the distribution of power in the world
and our position in it are not hard to imagine. Is it reasonable to
suppose that the Russians can continue to grow in the future at
the high rates achieved in the past? Does the deceleration of
growth in recent years augur a real turning point in this economic
rivalry or is it a temporary aberration that will be overcome? To
deal with this question it will perhaps be useful first to draw
together various parts of our explanation for past Soviet growth.
Some elements of the strategy, such as technological borrowing
and a high rate of investment, have already been discussed but
what we want to do here is to put all these elements together as
a coherent strategy of development and to explain its embodiment
in Soviet institutions.

Soviet growth is due partly to the fact that the Soviet leaders
have designed their system to achieve growth at the expense of
other objectives. The various objectives of an economic system,
such as welfare, growth, consumer satisfaction, and efficiency, are

to some extent mutually incompatible. The balance achieved among
them is influenced by economic organization. A set of institutions
and policies growing out of an extreme concern with welfare or
equity considerations may impede growth and allocational efficiency. Emphasis on growth may lead to allocational disarray in
the short run — bottlenecks with attendant shortages and surpluses,
irrational investments, and so on. An economy such as the American economy, with its great stress on pleasing the consumer, may
fail to grow as rapidly as production constraints by themselves
would make possible. The Russians have designed a system for
planning and coordinating their economy that is conducive to
growth but not especially well-suited to achieving some of these
other goals.

From an organizational point of view, the most distinctive aspect
of the Soviet economy is not that it is "socialist" or that its objectives are defined by the regime rather than by the population but
rather that all of this is implemented by what has been called a
"command economy." The variables of the economic system, such
as the quantity of each commodity produced and its disposition by
use, are largely determined by a set of detailed and explicit commands expressed in physical terms rather than by considerations
of price or accounting measures of profit. This kind of organization
permits the central planners to emphasize certain priorities and, to
the extent they can be expressed simply and starkly, to enforce
them stringently. It is a system of management in which every
executor is sensitive to and bound by priorities as passed down the
administrative hierarchy. By the same token managers are unre-
sponsive to lateral pressure, either from other producers or from
consumers, and are heedless of the more subtle implications of
their actions for the rest of the economy. The command economy
implies a considerable de-emphasis of money, price, financial
mechanisms, and controls. The behavior and decisions of lower
level administrators do not depend on conventional accounting
profit or necessarily on cost. The Russians retain money as a necessary element of their economic system but the power of money
has been considerably eroded. In market economies money is
power and distributes power. In the Soviet economy, however, the
power of money to command resources and influence decisions is

often frustrated when it comes into conflict with explicit physical commands and nonfinancial measures of success.

Another feature of Soviet economic organization is a distinctive distribution of power. The centralization of power in the hands of the regime rather than of consumers and its retention in the hands of the top leadership rather than its devolution to lower executive levels have already been mentioned. In addition, the locus of power over specific kinds of decisions often differs from the situation in our economy. The Russians have put power in the hands of those who can use it for growth and have kept it out of the hands of those who might use it for other purposes. For instance, management has very great power relative to labor on such issues as wages, technological change, or working conditions. The Soviet economy has been a "sellers' market" — in which the interests of sellers are served at the expense of the interests of buyers. Because of this circumstance no producer need ever be concerned with disposing of his output — an important factor serving to concentrate attention on the problem of increasing production. If in the American corporation the voice of those who represent marketing interests or financial interests often prevails over those whose specialty is production, the opposite is true in the Soviet firm. As between traditionalists and innovators, the former have usually been given the upper hand in the U.S.S.R. The planners do not want people with new or unorthodox ideas to interfere with the operations of those who will adhere to tried and true methods.

A third feature of the Soviet growth model has been sweeping economic judgments made at a high level and not subject to local adaptation or frequent change. For example, at an early stage of Soviet development it was decided to emphasize coal as the main energy source and to downgrade oil and gas. This judgment, probably uneconomic even at the time, became worse as time passed but it was three decades before this strategic decision was seriously re-evaluated. The same approach is evident in machinery design. During their whole history the Russians have produced only a few truck models and have completely omitted the production of some which would be very useful to them — such as small trucks. In agriculture it was decided to emphasize crawler tractors, especially large ones. Though these were satisfactory for large-scale combining and plowing operations, they were no answer to the large volume of lighter and more varied general work that exists in farming. In all branches of machine building the Russians have been reluctant to drop models that have been mastered and to replace them with more modern or more highly differentiated models. The most extreme form of this panacean approach has been in agriculture. Decisions about regional specialization, crop rotation schemes, choice of crops, organizational and technological decisions have often been uniform and extremist — in contradiction to the highly differentiated agricultural environment in which they were to be applied. The Williams grass-field system, with its exclusive emphasis on fallowing as the key to raising crop yields, Stalin's "plan for the transformation of nature," the virgin lands project, and the current campaigns for fertilizer use and irrigation are characteristic examples.

The system of success indicators described earlier reflects the policy of sweeping generalizations. Isolated elements of managerial performance have been singled out as the main criteria for guiding and evaluating managerial behavior.

These features of the strategy often have strong dysfunctional aspects and it may seem paradoxical to describe them as sources of growth. Nevertheless, it is probably true that this complex of organizational and policy decisions offered many advantages in achieving growth in the situation in which the Russians found themselves at the beginning of their industrialization period. It has handled very well some of the problems that plague other economic development efforts. For example, one of the greatest problems in any industrializing country is to transform traditional attitudes and inculcate new ways and new values. All the actors in the economic drama must abandon pre-industrial traditions and values in favor of the discipline and rational behavior of an urbanized, industrial economy. The command economy placed power and resources in the hands of those who were dedicated to imposing the new vision. By making the use of resources insensitive to the wishes of the population, it succeeded in reallocating resources in the direction of investment — one of the great problems confronting any industrializing country. Concentration on a limited number of equipment models and the reluctance to accept differentiation and rapid change probably saved more in resources through simplifying development and production problems than it cost through providing users with equipment imperfectly suited to their needs. That the cost of such changes is not small is indicated by the tremendous bill for model changes presented to the consumer in our own economy by the automobile industry, amounting to several billion dollars each year. Finally, the command principle and centralization helped bypass the obstacle of scarcity of managerial talent and technical ability. A system of centralized decisions on technical solutions and priorities passed down by explicit commands meant less stringent requirements in the way of local vision, initiative, and knowledge. It was a system which worked by "routinizing growth processes." As someone once characterized a military organization, the Soviet-type economy is a system "designed by geniuses to be run by idiots." Growth has been the result of following the routines laid out in Moscow rather than of conscientiously and consciously referring each little decision to the criterion of what its effect on growth would be. Probably the weakest part of the system was its inability to stimulate technological progress on a ubiquitous and continuous basis. Nevertheless, even here routinization enabled the system to skim off easy gains in technological progress. Many small-scale technological improvements were overlooked and many opportunities for slight upgrading as time went on were ignored by those who issued sweeping judgments on investment allocation and technological decision making but the routine application of a few important innovations at the margin continuously upgraded the average technological level of Soviet industry and the productivity of resources.

This interpretation of past Soviet growth might suggest that the Russians have created a growth machine which can simply grind on and on, producing growth routinely. Though this has been quite a common view, recent experience and thought have cast some doubt on it. There is an alternative view which stresses that as the Soviet economy has grown, it has changed — as has the nature of the growth problem. The success of the growth strategy so far has meant not only growth but also transformation. In becoming larger, the Soviet economy has become also more complex, has found itself face to face with new tasks and objectives, and has reached a level of technological maturity very different from that it exhibited when the process started. The kind of organization that will best promote growth probably changes as the nature of an economy changes, and the growth strategy which has been so effective in the past is apparently becoming less and less effective in this new environment. The deficiencies of the traditional Soviet model are likely to show up more emphatically today and tomorrow than in the past and its strengths are likely to find less and less applicability in the new situation.

The changing nature of the problem of achieving growth as total output increases and with the approach of technological maturity can be explained in terms of both aspects of the planning job — coordination and decision making.

The coordination job consists of making sure that the activities of different units in the system are consistent with each other, for example, that the quantity of a given material in the input program of one unit coincides with the output program of another or that the work of a research and development organization on some innovation is timed to coincide with the production scheduling of the industry which is to introduce it. Because of the growth of the Soviet economy, the number of firms whose actions must be coordinated is much greater today than it was in the past. For example, in industry the Gosplan today must coordinate the actions of over 200 thousand important firms, as against perhaps 20 thousand at the beginning of the thirties. More important, *the number of interactions among enterprises grows much faster than their number*. The number of possible pairs of enterprises, for example, grows as the square of the number of enterprises. The increase by ten times in the number of enterprises thus probably involves a growth in the amount of coordination work more nearly like one hundred times. The burden of handling the bulk of these interactions at the center threatens to become intolerable.

The problem of rational decision making increases in complexity because of the increasing range of choice and the greater number of alternatives to be considered in any decision. This is partly a question of technological modernity, partly a question of scale, and partly a matter of the world state of technology. At the beginning of Soviet industrialization, technological backwardness, shortages of skilled personnel, and lack of industrial capacity in crucial areas greatly narrowed the technological choices open to the Russians for dealing with any particular problem. Today many of those individual bottleneck limitations are removed and choices must be made from a much more confusing list of feasible alternatives. The fuel industry is an instructive example. In the thirties the fuel planners did consider a variety of alternative fuel mixes, locational patterns, and transportation alternatives. Many of them were ruled out, however, primarily on grounds that they were not feasible technologically. The Soviet planners limited their solutions to a relatively few sources of supply, a small number of transport methods, and a few possible utilization patterns. In discussions of fuel policy in the 1950's, when the subject was once again taken up, they found many more possibilities open to them. Pipelines are now technologically feasible; electric power can be transmitted over much longer distances today than it could be thirty years ago; they have discovered many more resources (especially of oil and gas) than they knew existed in the early thirties. These changes greatly increase the complexity of the problem of regionalization of energy production and consumption. In expanding the output of crude oil, greater geological knowledge and the development of more sophisticated geophysical methods have expanded the prospective hunting grounds. To rotary and cable tool drilling the Russians have added the new techniques of electric drilling and turbodrilling. In choosing an output mix for the petroleum industry and deciding on internal combustion engine design, a much broader range of possibilities is available today than in 1930. There are many more kinds of engines and the degree of control over the specifications of refinery products is now much greater.

Finally, the growth in consumption levels which has accompanied growth of GNP poses new problems. If in the past the planners could limit their planning of consumer goods output to a short list of basic items, they must now begin to consider a much wider variety and must balance improvements in quality, design, convenience, and consumer appeal against mere increases in quantity. The growth of incomes frees consumers from a kind of biological compulsion in deciding what they want and this means a need for more flexible and responsive planning of consumer goods output.

The thesis, in short, is that in this new situation the deficiencies of the old system become immensely magnified and its virtues cease to be so attractive. Changes in the environment of planning have made the traditional Soviet approach to growth obsolete. The traditional system is weak in two respects that have come to be ever more crucial, i.e., in the area of economic calculation and in the area of lateral communication.

The Soviet system is ill-suited for effective economic calculation, first of all because too much decision-making power is reserved to the center. Direct commands from the center leave the local decision maker too little freedom of choice. The exigencies of physical allocation and of direct physical command may not leave room for economic calculation. Even within the degree of freedom which the decision maker has for maneuver, he finds that the information on which he must base his decision is likely to be an unreliable basis for decisions. Because the administered price system of the Soviet economy is likely to be misleading as to the relative costs and benefits of the resources he consumes and produces, he cannot trust simple methods of calculation. For instance, in the oil industry there has long been a controversy concerning the economic effectiveness of measures designed to increase the output of oil from an existing field. Some authors suggest that these decisions be made by comparing the cost of producing an incremental ton with its price. Others, however, argue that the price of a ton of oil is no real measure of its worth to the national economy and that such a comparison of costs and benefits will not give a reliable answer as to whether the action should be taken.

Perhaps even more fundamental then either of these institutional limitations to rational decision making is the fact that Russian economists are still groping toward an understanding of the problem of calculation and allocation. The Marxian theory of value is deficient in failing to illuminate the integral relationship of value with the problem of allocation. Lacking an adequate theory of value and allocation, Soviet economists have a hard time seeing how institutions might be remodeled to eliminate the present obstacles to efficient allocation and purposeful calculation. As we will see below, there is now an elite among Soviet economists who are remarkably conversant with modern economic theory. But sophisticated appreciation of the basic ideas of value and allocation is still not widespread.

Closely related to these weaknesses is the difficulty in the Soviet economy of getting adequate lateral communication between producing units. In a market economy the power of money and prices gives every economic actor a way of directly influencing the actions of others. The Soviet system has abrogated the power of money to a large degree and replaced it with authority residing in the higher levels of a pyramidal administrative structure. In such a system the only means of influencing another economic unit is to go up through the hierarchy until one finds a common boss, that is, a node of authority with jurisdiction over your unit and the one you want to influence. In the command economy economic actors are accountable only to their superiors in the hierarchy and so can only be influenced "through channels." Unfortunately, this common boss may be so high up the hierarchy that communication with him and any hope of exerting influence on him is drowned out in the channels of communication. The point can be illustrated with several examples. A Soviet truck designer trying to explain why for years on end there had been no improvement in the quality of the trucks produced by his plant tells the following story. The truck model now in production has serious design failures which have not been corrected since the beginning of production soon after World War II. For instance, the engine block castings are not properly cured and, after being machined and assembled into engines, they continue to change slightly in size, violating the original tolerances to which they were machined. The result is excessive wear and expensive maintenance for the organizations using the trucks. The design department of the truck plant has figured out ways to eliminate this problem. Though such measures would raise the cost of producing the engine slightly, the extra cost would be recouped many times over in maintenance savings to the truck users. Whenever the design department proposed these changes, however, the director of the truck plant would not agree to them. Under the Soviet price system, such quality improvements would not be reflected in higher prices for the trucks and so there would be no improvement in the output indicator which is so important in evaluating success and giving bonuses. The extra costs *would* show up, however, as worsened performance in another important indicator — cost — and the director does not want to jeopardize his premia.

In the market economy, competition and the dependence of the manufacturer on his customers' wishes would soon lead to the introduction of the desired changes. But in the Soviet-type economy the only way the truck users could influence this decision would be by appeal to a common boss who would recognize the validity of the request for improvement from the point of national economic efficiency and order the truck producer to make the change. In this case, obviously, the common boss would not be found anywhere short of the very top level of executive authority in the Soviet economy. But because there are so many such questions, this level of authority is overburdened with issues such as this one to resolve. Also, when such questions get to the higher echelons they may seem so petty that they are not taken seriously or so complicated that people in authority shy away from getting them resolved.

The Russians have experimented with many techniques for dealing with this problem of lateral communication. One is to group operating units so that those who regularly deal with each other will find themselves under common bosses at a relatively low level. In the oil industry, for example, the oil producers have always tried to have research organizations, oil field machinery producers, and exploratory activities under their own jurisdiction. Their mutual interactions can thus be coordinated without their having to go all the way to the top. Similarly, the industrial reorganization of 1957 was an attempt to regroup organizations so that those which had important dealings with each other on matters of subcontracting and specialization would find themselves under the jurisdiction of a relatively close and accessible boss in the regional economic council. That approach, however, can never really solve the problem because the economic connections of any unit radiate in many directions and embrace many other kinds of organizations. The dilemma here is well illustrated in a discussion by a Soviet writer concerned with who should have jurisdiction over the construction machinery industry. For efficient, low-cost production of this machinery it would be desirable to put the plants under the boss of the machinery industry, i.e., together with plants that employed similar technology, were subject to the same kind of standardization procedures, etc. On the other hand, the writer held that the only way to make these plants sensitive to the needs of the *users* of construction machinery in questions of design, variety and quality would be to put them under the jurisdiction of the construction industry. They must be put in one place or the other and either alternative would de-emphasize attention to an important consideration.

The response of any western economist to this catalog of difficulties is a recommendation to restore the power of money, place more emphasis on prices, free decision makers from detailed commands, phrase the orders transmitted to them and evaluate their performance in terms of value measures. This would make it possible for lower-level decision makers to consider the full range of alternatives, while prices and money would provide the means by which each unit could influence the actions of those with whom it had to act in concert.

The novel thing about Soviet economic thought today is that a diagnosis and prescription much like this seems to have been accepted by Russian economists and the Russian leaders themselves. As we have already related in Chapters 3 and 5, the suggestion of E. G. Liberman that an enterprise should be freed from "petty tutelage" by higher-level bureaucrats and judged only by its profit results elicited so favorable a response from managers that "Libermanism" has become an articulate and influential movement. The leadership has now responded with far-reaching moves in the direction of widening enterprise autonomy and judging success by profit performance. Whether these reforms really go far enough to unshackle the Soviet economy and turn its present wastes into a potential for renewed growth is difficult to say. It has already been suggested that for all their boldness these reforms represent a kind of halfway house on the road to complete decentralization and market control and that this may jeopardize their success. The experience of some of the Eastern European countries is highly suggestive here. Yugoslavia after its break with the Soviet Union in 1948 radically restructured its economic system to abolish command planning and to replace it with market controls, even going so far as to auction capital resources among potential investors on a competitive basis with the use of an interest rate and to permit almost complete local autonomy in economic decision making. Though the results were generally satisfactory, the Yugoslav economy showed some severe strains in the early sixties in the form of inflation and resource misallocation which some Yugoslav economists have rather convincingly explained as resulting from not having gone quite far enough. The Czechs, too, have undertaken an economic reform to combat inefficiencies and a deceleration of growth which reached alarming proportions in the early sixties. The proponents of this reform argued that it would be fruitless unless it went all the way and won support for this idea. The Russian leaders apparently have not been convinced that so radical a measure of change is required and are trying to move away from centralized planning a few steps at a time. It is quite clear that the first experimental steps toward the system of direct ties and profit incentives (in the textile and apparel industries) were made in response to an emergency situation. Soviet consumers had simply ceased to buy the output of textile and clothes factories and it was piling up in warehouses in amounts to rival the agricultural surpluses of the United States. The need to cope with this emergency was the entering wedge of Libermanism and, although it has now been extended further in the 1965 reforms, the leaders still understand only partially the rationale of a price system and market forces as regulators of enterprise behavior and they let go of the strings of direct control only grudgingly.

But the basis for a more sophisticated understanding of how to reconcile central control with local decision making has now been solidly established by a new elite of mathematical economists inspired by the work of L. V. Kantorovich and V. V. Novozhilov. In the writings of these men, the Russians have at long last been provided with a set of ideas that will enable them to think analytically about the problem of calculation and allocation. Kantorovich and Novozhilov have seen clearly and stated convincingly for their colleagues the basic insight that scarcity requires efficient allocation among alternative uses and that, out of the process of balancing off resource use for alternative purposes, there emerges a set of values for all resources. Since this crucial insight is simply missing in Marxian economic theory, it was very difficult for Soviet economists even to conceptualize that the command approach to coordination and allocation could be replaced by a system of prices and decentralized decision making. The significance of values or prices is that they provide the link that makes parochial efforts at calculation consistent with national economic efficiency and thus they open the way to effective decentralized economic decision making. Though the effect of Kantorovich's ideas on Soviet intellectual history and on Soviet ideology is far reaching, we are interested here primarily in how he tries to apply this theory of value to the operation of a planned economy. Generally speaking, his recommendations sound like "market socialism." He sees that value offers an opportunity to scrap the main feature of the command economy, i.e., detailed direction of every economic performer in favor of indirect control over their actions through value indicators. If the worth and cost of all economic goods can be found, then it will be possible to let producers make their own decisions, requiring only that whatever they do, the cost of what they use should not exceed the value of what they produce. The "new economics" of the Kantorovich school may thus reinforce the pressure of events to lead the Russians to a thoroughgoing market-style reform.

On the other hand, the recent Soviet discussion of mathematical methods in economics also contains a second theme and a different vision of how the Soviet economy might cope with its organizational crisis. This alternative vision has been most energetically propounded by the late V. S. Nemchinov who proposed to employ the new sophistication concerning value and allocation and the new data processing potentials offered by computers to determine optimum *quantities* rather than equilibrium prices. The Gosplan would then use the computer output as the traditional orders of the command economy — but made perfect and rational. In this vision, the computer with its great advantage over human beings in its ability to absorb and employ information, will rejuvenate the principle of a command economy even in the contemporary, more complex setting. The situation is analogous to that of large firms in the western world, firms which at one point decentralized such functions as inventory control — because of the clumsiness of trying to handle them in the head office — but which have since found that with modern data processing capacity such functions can be centralized once again.

To summarize, there may be more than one way out of the organizational crisis. Of these two visions, the latter is no doubt more congenial to the Russian leadership. The idea of giving up the familiar instruments by which they have controlled the economy, and relying instead on the indirect techniques of manipulating prices, profits, taxes, and credit, no doubt frightens them. On the other hand, there are articulate forces in the society who favor the decentralized answer and there are some strong arguments against the feasibility of the computerized Utopia. It would take a foolhardy prophet to predict which alternative will win out; there seems little doubt that this will be a continuing and unresolved issue for some time to come. The inclination of the author is to say that the decentralized version must win out — there are too many obstacles to the effective operation of the computerized Utopia.

This leaves unsettled the real issue as to whether a rapid rate of growth can continue. The argument is that, even with considerable decentralization, the economy can be made to serve centralized ends and the leadership can still guide the new system to serve the aim of rapid growth. Also, it has been suggested that if present wastes can be captured and the presently imprisoned initiative released, if these misallocations and wrong decisions can be ameliorated, then the limits to growth on the supply side will widen to make possible a continuation at high rates and so decentralization by itself may not mean deceleration.

To get at this issue, we need to look at one more aspect of the question. One important influence on the outcome is likely to be the question of drive, the will to growth on the part of the leadership. The Soviet growth machine generates tremendous social tension. It substitutes a central vision for a social consensus concerning the goals of economic policy, especially in its emphasis on postponement of higher consumption in favor of serving other purposes first. This situation demands on the part of those who proclaim the vision assurance that they are right and a clear sense of the objectives that underlie their policies. In the past the definition of the goal was simple — to catch up with the more advanced capitalist countries. For a long time this was so distant an objective that it could have a kind of celestial purity, fixity, and ultimateness. Although the Russians have not by any means caught up with the United States in overall productive capacity, there are some areas in which today they match our levels of output and other areas in which they are getting close as shown in the preceding chapters. Once so remote that it seemed self-sufficient and immutable, the goal of catching up has now come close enough to be examined more carefully. The leadership must clarify for themselves the ultimate destination toward which this milestone leads. In the process may it not happen that the leadership will become less confident in its vision and less willing to impose the tension imposed for its sake in the past? The analytical tools of the economist do not really prepare him to deal with this question but it is one that can scarcely be ignored in thinking about the future of the Soviet economy.

It should be stressed that it is not so much that the population will be asking — "Now that we are catching up, why do we have to keep working so hard at it?" They have asked that all along. The real novelty today is that the leadership has no clear answer. The history of the past 30 years suggests that the Communist leadership has not been very imaginative or convincing in propounding a vision of social purpose or of what constitutes the "good life." Communist morality, socialist realism in art, Marxian versions of Utopia have never really enlisted the loyalty of the Soviet populace. This is one reason why the masses in communist countries are so easily infected with western cultural influences. With catching up becoming less an end in itself and more a means to some other end, the leadership may become demoralized and susceptible to all kinds of pressures for slowing down. Certainly one can detect already a very serious shift in priorities toward emphasizing consumption as opposed to other possible uses of resources. This was a persistent theme in the speeches of Khrushchev, especially in the later years of his power. More and more people have been posing, in effect, the classic question — "What is the point of making more steel to make more steel mills to make more steel forever and ever if we are never to get washing machines and refrigerators?" Khrushchev and his successors have also been quite explicit in saying that one of the important goals of the 1965–70 plan should be significant increases in the levels of consumption. This is the kind of talk for which people might have been liquidated in the past but to such reversals of behavior does economic development lead. The conflict with the Chinese and the potency of this argument in creating a humanistic and rational image for the Soviet Union have greatly hastened its adoption, of course.

This erosion of the will to growth will not take place overnight; it is the kind of subtle and slow transformation that takes much longer to work itself out. Nevertheless, it is one of the contingencies that we should be prepared to think about. There is a danger that because it is an attractive "solution" to the Soviet threat, we may be beguiled into seeing it when it is not there. It must be labeled clearly a hypothesis to be checked against the facts as they actually develop. But it seems a realistic possibility, the consequences of which would probably include a slowdown in the rate of growth.

Suggestions for Further Reading

The discussions in the text have constituted only an introduction to the subject of the operation and performance of the Soviet economy. Many qualifications and interesting details have necessarily been omitted, and many problems were not even mentioned because of the limitations of space. But for the sake of the interested reader, a list of works in English that might be consulted for more information on some of the problems covered is included. Considerations of how widely available a source might be and how completely each one covered a subject of general interest guided the selection. Because extensive research on the Soviet economy is a fairly recent enterprise, much of the literature in the field is still in the form of journal articles. Useful collections of these have now appeared as books of readings, for example, Franklyn D. Holzman, *Readings on the Soviet Economy* (Rand McNally, 1962), Morris Bornstein and Daniel Fusfeld, *The Soviet Economy, A Book of Readings* (Irwin, 1962), and Harry Shaffer, *The Soviet Economy, A Collection of Western and Soviet Views* (Appleton-Century-Crofts, 1963). Each of these contains a more or less comprehensive coverage of the whole range of problems the Soviet economy presents, and between them they contain most of the best articles that have appeared in this field. Another general introduction, with an approach sufficiently different from the present book to make it a useful complement, is Alec Nove, *The Soviet Economy* (Praeger, 1961).

Two general works which survey Soviet development chronologically and include extended discussion of the early years are Maurice Dobb, *Soviet Economic Development since 1917* (International Publishers, 1948) and Naum Jasny, *Soviet Industrialization, 1928–1952* (University of Chicago Press, 1961). The first is an account sympathetic to Soviet interpretations and justifications of growth policies, the second is much more sceptical of official Soviet claims and interpretations. A more specialized study of the industrialization debates, and the one on which the discussion in Chapter 2 has drawn extensively, is Alexander Erlich, *The Soviet Industrialization Debate, 1924–1928* (Harvard University Press, 1960). The early debates concerning strategy and planning methods for economic development are also surveyed in Nicolas Spulber, *Soviet Strategy for Economic Growth* (Indiana University Press, 1964). A companion volume, *Foundations of Soviet Strategy for Economic Growth* (Indiana University Press, 1964), contains a selection of Soviet writings from this period which are extremely valuable for conveying concretely the intensity and the imagination that went into these controversies.

Reading a Soviet textbook on planning is a good way to see how the Russians conceptualize planning and the procedures and institutions by which it is effected. One such text available in English translation is I. A. Evenko, *Planning in the USSR* (Foreign Language Publishing House, 1961). General theoretical conceptualizations by outsiders of the essential features of the Soviet decision-making and allocational system are Robert Campbell, "On the Theory of Economic Administration" in Henry Rosovsky, *Industrialization in Two Systems* (Wiley, 1966), and Gregory Grossman, "Notes for a Theory of the Command Economy," *Soviet Studies,* October, 1963. A detailed description of the Soviet approach to the balancing problem, together with institutional description of the planning agencies involved, may be found in two articles by Herbert Levine, "The Centralized Planning of Supply in Soviet Industry," (available in both the Holzman and the Bornstein and Fusfeld readings books) and "Recent Developments in Soviet Planning," in U.S. Congress, Joint Economic Committee, *Dimensions of Soviet Economic Power* (USGPO, 1962). This latter volume, incidentally, is also a very useful compendium of the current views and knowledge of Soviet economic conditions among specialists on the Soviet economy as of 1962. Soviet experimentation with input-output methods is described, and one of the tables the Russians have produced is reconstructed by Vladimir Treml in an appendix in U.S. Congress, Joint Economic Committee, *Annual Economic Indicators for the USSR* (USGPO, 1964).

For an excellent discussion of the Soviet capital allocation controversy, see Gregory Grossman, "Scarce Capital and Soviet Doctrine," *Quarterly Journal of Economics,* August, 1953 (also available in the Holzman readings book). There have been important further developments in Soviet thought and practice on capital allocation since the publication of that article, and these were summed up in a conference sponsored by the Institute of Economics of the USSR Academy of Science. A report of the discussions at this conference is available in English translation in *Problems of Economics,* Vol. I, No. 9. This journal contains full translations of important theoretical Soviet articles in economics. (The translation is published by the International Arts and Sciences Press, 108 Grand St., White Plains, New York.) Reading a few issues of this journal is a good way to get some idea of what Soviet economists talk about, the quality of their economic theorizing, and so on. A detailed study of the location decisions in the iron and steel industry is contained in M. Gardner Clark, *The Economics of Soviet Steel* (Cambridge, 1957), and a more specialized discussion of problems of rationality in location decisions is found in Franklyn D. Holzman, "The Soviet Ural-Kuznetsk Combine," *Quarterly Journal of Economics,* August, 1957.

The problems of lower level decision making and incentives at the level of the firm have been widely discussed in the Soviet press in the last several years, and this discussion is full of fascinating examples of the irrationalities that the system encourages, and some rather bold suggestions for possible reforms. Access to this kind of material is easy through the *Current Digest of the Soviet Press,* published by the Joint Committee on Slavic Studies. This is a weekly publication containing English translations of important speeches, articles, and documents appearing in the Soviet press. It is available in many libraries in this country. It is an excellent source of current information on Soviet affairs, and reading through a few issues of it is a wonderful way to obtain an impression of what the Soviet press is like.

Two interesting studies of management are Joseph Berliner, *Factory and Manager in the USSR* (Harvard University Press, 1957) and David Granick, *Management of the Industrial Firm in the USSR* (Columbia University Press, 1954).

Abram Bergson, *The Structure of Soviet Wages* (Harvard University Press, 1944) is a study of the principles underlying Soviet wage policy, and actual practice in wage differentiation as these emerged in the thirties. The wartime restrictions on labor mobility, along with many other aspects of Soviet labor policy, are covered in Solomon Schwarz, *Labor in the Soviet Union* (Praeger, 1953). Each of the readings books mentioned earlier has a section on labor, and these include discussions of the postwar wage reforms and dismantling of coercive labor legislation.

The changes in agricultural policy since the death of Stalin reveal a complex history. In this area, too, there has been a great deal of public discussion of problems and proposals, for which the *Current Digest* is an excellent source. Khrushchev's numerous speeches on agricultural problems are an essential part of this record, and many of them are available there. Nancy Nimitz has published two excellent surveys of Soviet agriculture. One, in U.S. Congress, Joint Economic Committee, *Comparisons of the U.S. and Soviet Economies,* Part I (USGPO, 1959), is a masterful analysis of the debacle to which Stalinist policies had led agriculture at the time of his death. The other covers the period of Khrushchev's dominance in agricultural policy, with an interpretation of his successes and failures — "Russia's Lean Years," *Problems of Communism* (May-June, 1965). Another such survey is Jerzy Karcz and V. P. Timoshenko, "Soviet Agricultural Policy," *Food Research Institute Studies,* Vol. IV, No. 2, 1964. A full-length description of the economics of Soviet agriculture, including a discussion of its performance, is found in Naum Jasny, *The Collectivized Agriculture of the USSR* (Stanford University Press, 1949).

The findings of the research on Soviet growth carried out by Abram Bergson and his associates for the RAND Corporation are scattered in a large number of publications. But two works are especially important—Abram Bergson, *The Real National Income of Soviet Russia since 1928* (Harvard University Press, 1961), and Abram Bergson and Simon Kuznets, *Economic Trends in the Soviet Union* (Harvard University Press, 1963). The first contains Bergson's conclusions on growth of Soviet GNP and its various components. The second, consisting of the papers given at a conference, contains more interpretation and comparisons with the historical experience of other countries.

The sources for the indexes of Soviet industrial growth in Table 6 are G. Warren Nutter, *Growth of Industrial Production in the Soviet Union* (Princeton University Press, 1962); Donald Hodgman, *Soviet Industrial Production, 1928–51* (Harvard University Press, 1954); Norman Kaplan and Richard Moorsteen, "An Index of Soviet Industrial Output," *American Economic Review,* June, 1960 (also reprinted in the Holzman readings book); Naum Jasny, *The Soviet Economy during the Plan Era* (Stanford University Press, 1951), and Rush Greenslade and Phyllis Wallace, "Industrial Production in the USSR" in U.S. Congress, Joint Economic Committee, *Dimensions of Soviet Economic Power* (USGPO, 1962) (this index is extended to later years in the JEC *Annual Economic Indicators* volume of 1964). Hodgman's study was one of the first of the western recomputations and contains an excellent discussion of the rationale for such recomputations.

Most of the productivity comparisons made in Chapter 7 are computed from data in the basic statistical handbooks of the two countries, which are too detailed and specialized to warrant listing here. But mention should be made of the *Statistical Abstract of the United States,* published annually by the U.S. Department of Commerce. This is a convenient and very complete reference for any kind of statistics on the United States. It also contains suggestions of where to find additional statistical information.

Several of the Soviet statistical handbooks are available in English translation, and are essential for any more detailed study of the Soviet economy. The most general one is Central Statistical Administration, *The National Economy of the USSR,* published in several editions.

Studies of the economics of individual sectors of the Soviet economy often contain Soviet-U.S. productivity comparisons, as for example, Walter Galenson, *Labor Productivity in Soviet and American Industry* (Columbia University Press, 1954); Holland

Hunter, *Soviet Transportation Policy* (Harvard University Press, 1957); M. Gardner Clark, *The Economics of Soviet Steel* (Harvard University Press, 1955); Demitri Shimkin, *The Soviet Mineral-fuels Industries, 1928–1958* (USGPO, 1963); and Ernest Williams, *Freight Transportation in the Soviet Union, Including Comparisons with the United States* (Princeton University Press, 1962).

Interesting studies concerned with interpreting the Soviet growth process in the light of its institutional arrangements include Gregory Grossman, "Soviet Growth, Routine, Inertia and Pressure," *American Economic Review,* May, 1960, and David Joravsky, "The Lysenko Affair," *Scientific American,* November, 1962. The relationship of educational policy to economic growth is surveyed in Nicholas DeWitt, *Education and Professional Employment in the USSR* (USGPO, 1961). The revolution in economic theory, stimulated by the work of Kantorovich and Novozhilov and the doctrinal problems involved, are analyzed in Robert Campbell, "Marx, Kantorovich and Novozhilov, *Stoimost'* versus Reality," *Slavic Review,* October, 1961. Kantorovich's major work on optimum resource use has now been translated and published as *The Best Use of Economic Resources* (Harvard University Press, 1965). One can also sample the quality of Novozhilov's thinking in a piece in the recently translated volume edited by V. S. Nemchinov, *The Use of Mathematics in Economics,* Oliver and Boyd, 1964.

Index

DATE

MAR 1 2 2000

DEMCO, INC. 38-2971